Reset

Reset:

The Playbook
to Transform *All*
Parenting Relationships

MARK L. BRENNER

Copyright © 2019 Mark L. Brenner. All rights reserved.

No part of this book may be reproduced or transmitted in any form or by any means, electronic or mechanical, including photocopying, recording, broadcast or by any information storage or retrieval system, without written permission from Mark L. Brenner, MFT, Ph.D., except for the inclusion of other authors' quotations or works referenced.

Library of Congress Control Number: 2019903332

ISBN# 978-0-9708766-0-7

Dr. Mark L. Brenner is one of the most respected Marriage and Family therapists and parenting experts in the field of early childhood development, adolescence and high-conflict family issues. Known as *The Family Whisperer,* Dr. Brenner helps families make stunning changes and is one of the few family therapists who also makes house calls.

He is the founder of the life changing workshops: *Parent Fitness Training*® and *Parenting Without Therapy*®. He works closely with many private and public schools, and is an adjunct professor at Pepperdine University where he teaches group therapy. Dr. Brenner is the author of *Raising an Adult, When No Gets You Nowhere and Pacifiers, Bottles & Thumbs.* He is also the author of *Tipping for Success,* the best book about tipping and how to get celebrity style service everywhere. Dr. Brenner is currently working on a new web and podcast series called, *"Open Session."* He can be reached at drmarklbrenner@att.net

For my Mom, who made everything possible.

Contents:

The Single Root Cause 1

The Five Parenting Rules 5

    RULE ONE: Show a Complete Understanding 9

    RULE TWO: Talk With Respect 43

    RULE THREE: Promote a Family Culture of Truth 63

    RULE FOUR: Enforce Consequences Consistently 89

    RULE FIVE: Express Unrelenting Optimism 109

The 60-Second Test 127

The Difficult Child 129

The Difficult Spouse 145

Technology and Social Media 163

Reset Tips 169

The Five Rules Summary 177

A Suggestion:

Congratulations, you're minutes away from learning how to reset a moment or your relationship. It's tempting to skip the next few pages and jump straight to the five rules. I encourage you to read these pages first, you'll get there faster!

All will be good.

MLB

May 2019

"But I like living in the past. It's where I grew up."

The Single Root Cause

All truth passes through three stages.
First, it is ridiculed.
Second, it is violently opposed.
Third, it is accepted as being self-evident.
—ARTHUR SCHOPENHAUER

In an effort to help parents reflect on the level of closeness they have with their children, I often ask the audience in the beginning of my workshops the following question: Are you here for *repair* or to *strengthen* the relationship with your child or teenager?

Most parents answer, "To strengthen."

One hour later, I ask the same question again. The new answer, "To repair."

Let's get right to it. The single root cause for all struggling parent-child relationships is the loss of emotional and/or physical trust. This loss develops because of a lack of consistency around nurturing issues such as the right doses of comfort, attention, nutrition, limit setting and an overall intuitive sense of knowing what to do or say during times of difficulty. On a fundamental level, children express a need for emotional connection and the

> The single root cause for all struggling parent-child relationships is the loss of emotional and/or physical trust

parent either satisfies those needs, tries and fails, or remains unaware that there was an emotional or physical need in the first place. The question then becomes to what degree those vital needs go unmet. This lack of consistent emotional trust stays with us throughout childhood and well beyond. It is the core cause of relationship problems.

While these unmet needs can serve as a huge motivational driver to prove or achieve status and success later in life, they more often lead to self-destructive personal behaviors, unhealthy relationships and social isolation. These are risk factors that can be avoided.

In every parent-child relationship, actually in all relationships, at some point we find ourselves saying, "Can we start over again? We need a reset." Sometimes we need a simple reset in the moment, sometimes we need one because of built-up tensions over days, weeks or months, and sometimes we discover a deeper truth and need to repair the relationship. When we reach those conflict points, we often think, "I wish there was a playbook of what to do?"

When our primary relationships become conflicted, we feel more alone, more angry and more fearful. As we get older it becomes easier to trust someone with our finances, our spiritual beliefs, even our bodies, rather than to risk once again our deepest feelings. In an effort to continue self-protection, we have learned to create walls for a danger that has long past. As a result, people suffer with these walls their whole life.

The real challenge in parenting shouldn't be the relationship. That should be

> The real challenge in parenting shouldn't be the relationship. That should be the easy part. The real challenge and privilege is to identify each child's in-born struggles and talents and know just how to help

The Single Root Cause

> These rules satisfies our three most important relationship needs:
>
> Understand me,
>
> Accept me,
>
> Believe in me

the easy part. The real challenge and privilege is to identify each child's in-born struggles and talents and know just how to help.

It makes no difference if a child is average, gifted, perfectionist, brilliant, ADD, high-strung, anxious, defiant, lacking in motivation, socially awkward, has learning differences, on the spectrum, or has any other developmental issue. You can't help a child, or anyone else for that matter, if the relationship is strained or fractured. It's that simple.

With that in mind, I identify five parenting rules that resets emotional trust and delivers a powerful and permanent antidote to repair all parenting relationships. It doesn't matter what difficulties or stage of life your child or teenager is going through. These rules are indigenous to intact families, step-families, blended-families, single-parents, adoptive-families, or any other loving combination. A child can struggle of course, but the relationship shouldn't. These rules satisfies our three most important relationship needs: *Understand me, Accept me, Believe in me.*

RESET is an evolutionary parenting approach that requires wearing three different hats: One as **the head coach**, modeling unity, values and optimism; one as the **the sports announcer** giving a play-by-play description of what's happening in the moment; and one as **the ref**, making the call out-loud and saying the real truth when conflict arises.

The Five Parenting Rules

*It's not wise to violate rules
until you know how to observe them.*
—T. S. ELIOT

The five parenting rules are rooted in one unalterable axiom: *"When you change your response, you change your child's behavior."* As a result, children will acquire five vital life-skills: *Empathy, Self-Worth, Self-Awareness, Self-Control and Self-Confidence.*

Want another reason to follow the five parenting rules? Your child won't marry the wrong person. Why? Because they will have experienced what a satisfying and natural relationship really feels like.

Now these are rules worth following!

Rule One
Show a Complete Understanding

Rule Two
Talk With Respect

Rule Three
Promote a Family Culture of Truth

Rule Four
Enforce Consequences Consistently

Rule Five
Show Unrelenting Optimism

It helps to think of these parenting rules in the same way you would think about a diet or an exercise routine. I like this comparison because when we regularly exercise or diet, we have no illusions about what will happen when we stop. We never think that our strength, endurance and "fit" feeling will automatically continue. We know it won't. Miss just two weeks and you're already doing repair work. It's the same with relationships. Consistency is everything. The takeaway: *Don't stop when all is good.*

> Luck is not a parenting strategy

I discuss each parenting rule in three ways: First, I explain, *why they work.* Second, *how to communicate each one.* And third, I identify which life-skill your child will acquire as a result. Unlike many things in life in which there are an infinite number of ways for achieving the same results, with parenting I believe there's only one way. We shouldn't be guessing.

Luck is not a parenting strategy.

> *"Any fool can know.*
> *The point is to understand."*
>
> —ALBERT EINSTEIN

Rule One

SHOW A COMPLETE UNDERSTANDING

EMPATHY

"People don't care how much you know until they know how much you care."
—THEODORE ROOSEVELT

Experience tells us you can only help someone get over their feelings by helping them get through them, not around them. Kids are no different. A child who is upset and struggling should not be ignored or looked at with a dismissive or smiling face as though their experience is cute or annoying. At the same time, we can't go overboard and indulge every feeling. The challenge it seems is knowing at what level to show it? Without a consistent feeling of being shown that we are deeply understood, we are drawn to other connections and increase risky behaviors.

> Without a consistent feeling of being shown that we are deeply understood and respected, we are drawn to other connections and increase risky behaviors

Finding the right balance between acknowledging feelings and knowing how to get on with what must be done, is what parents struggle with.

"Lenny, you think I favor your sister Hannah. You think I let her get away with everything and it's not fair. You're sick of it! Tell me more."

"Henry, let's talk about how much you hate school."

It makes no difference if your child is two or twenty-two. In no way am I suggesting that we should elevate feelings above our behaviors. Not at all. I am saying that when we consistently bypass feelings, we can expect more power struggles. Rule one will not embolden your child, it will civilize him and build empathy.

At face value it can seem like an exhausting process to stay in the moment and talk through feelings, especially with little kids. A five year-old who's having a screaming tantrum because you don't have his favorite breakfast cereal, a middle schooler who won't start his homework on time, a teenager who thinks you're mean because you won't let him have the car. A parent's first thought, "I'm not going to conduct a 'therapy session' for every feeling for such ridiculousness; besides, it doesn't work anyway."

What prevents most parents from staying in the moment are two mistaken beliefs. The first is that the process will take too much time. It doesn't. In fact, after making this skill your default approach, it can take as little as ten-seconds, and typically no more than three minutes. The second mistaken belief about showing a complete understanding is that it will lead the other person to think that you're in agreement with what they're saying.

It also won't, although it may surprise you how many times you actually will agree. *What your child*

> **WHEN WE CONSISTENTLY BYPASS FEELINGS, WE CAN EXPECT MORE POWER STRUGGLES**

Rule One

or any adult is looking for during times of upset is not really agreement, but to be believed! They need for you to take their feelings seriously. You can't garner cooperation when you dismiss feelings on the spot.

What we crave is to be understood and believed. Without knowing how to express empathy, no relationship can ever feel natural or be satisfying. Each day will feel like the previous days battle with little cooperation. If we are completely honest with ourselves, feeling completely understood is much more satisfying than even being loved. You can be loved and not at all understood. But, when you are deeply understood, you always feel love.

What makes this so critical is that when you don't know how to fully show understanding to your child (or anyone else you care about), it is unlikely you will be the one they turn to when they need help with their life issues. My favorite enduring quote that captures this meaning fully, will take your breath away. It comes from the genius of Robin Williams (I'm still feeling his loss) in the movie, *World's Greatest Dad*.

"I used to think the worst thing in life was feeling alone. It's not. The worst thing in life is to end up with people who make you feel all alone."

For some, empathy comes naturally. Others struggle hard remembering to focus first on how the other person is feeling. It is not about you, your opinions, your childhood or your advice. *Like an acoustical soundboard, absorb what you see and hear before bouncing it back.* No minimizing, no dismissing, arguing or impatient facial expressions. Instead, mentally calibrate the level of upset or excitement your child is feeling so you can match it back when the time is right.

Even as you're reading this page it's tempting to think, "I get the point Brenner. Enough, move on already. Just give me the steps." It's the same when your child or teenager is trying to tell you something important. You think, "I got it. I don't need to hear anymore." The truth is, there's always a little more. It only takes a few quick minutes. You can't rush an emotional conversation. And, just like you will garner more insight about your child's behavior, not skipping these pages you will garner more critical understanding on why *Rule One* is rule one!

When you think about it, isn't that what experienced therapists do? A satisfying therapeutic relationship is valuable in part precisely because of a predictable experience of being both deeply understood and believed. Parenting is no different. Even when your child's feelings are misguided, you still must never dismiss out of hand what they are saying or showing. The comparison to a therapist may sound a bit dramatic for a parenting book, but it is a sobering truth that children have the same fundamental emotional needs as we do. Only when we are sincerely believed and taken seriously, do we begin to trust, relax and open-up. You don't have to agree with what you hear, but if you want to gain emotional trust and cooperation, you must sincerely communicate that you take your child seriously.

If you have any doubt just how important empathy is in a relationship, think about the different ways that you want to be physically touched at certain times, for example when you want to be relaxed, loved or in pain. When we are touched the wrong way, we withdraw, or get angry and turn-off.

Empathy is another form of touch

Empathy is another form of touch. It has to feel just right, or we recoil. Thinking about empathy as a form of touch makes it easier to to be warmhearted and gentle when it's time to respond.

FAKE LISTENING

No one wants to be just 'listened to' even though that's the common belief. Listening with no understanding is equivalent to being a good reader and missing the meaning in what you just read. It becomes an empty experience. The late author and wonderful educator Stephen Covey framed the process of conversation this way: "Most people do not listen with the intent to understand, they listen with the intent to reply." This is a life-changing insight!

This is why we need to resist the temptation to "fake listen" in order to say: "Yes, but…," along with its other equivalents such as "however" and "although." Those short 'but' responses signal to your child (or anyone else for that matter), "I'm only pretending to be interested in what you are saying. Now I'm going to tell you what I really think." Fake listening is like counterfeit money, they both have no value. Other fake listening responses that prevent emotional connection include, "I hear you," "okay," and "right." You can see this on television talk shows when a host tries to appear interested in what a guest is talking about and they say, "Right right," "Okay," or "I hear you." These are filler words to move a conversation along faster.

A far more satisfying way to show real interest and understanding is to respond with point of view conclusions. "I never looked at it like that." "That's so true." "That makes sense." "I'm not sure I understand." "Tell me more." These point of view responses show you are seriously following along and not just playing along. Nothing creates more distance between two people than fake listening. Imagine if you and I met at one of my workshops and you were telling me something you considered very important, but while you were talking I was looking at you with flat affect superficially saying, "Right, right," or "I hear you." What level of interest would you feel from me? Probably very little, or none at all.

In the context of relationships, the most important degrees in life are not

> **Most people do not listen with the intent to understand, they listen with the intent to reply**

> **Fake listening is like counterfeit money, they both have no value**

the academic PhDs, but the degrees in understanding. I have long believed that the education of the heart needs to keep pace with the education of the mind.

Too often, the common mistake is to starve the emotions in order to overfeed the intellect. Yet, we know a deeper truth: Out of the heart comes the real issues of life! Just as in nature, the blossom comes before the fruit, so in the child, emotions come before reason. Which is why more than 50 years ago, pioneering Psychologist Dr. Haim Ginott said, *"Fish swim, birds fly, and people feel!"* Our very basic emotions include joy, fear, surprise, sadness, anger, disgust and contempt.

A humorous story is told about a man who worked for a company for 18 years and not a single time was he ever late for work, not even once. *One morning he came in an hour late looking very badly bruised. His lip was swollen, his nose bloody and he had a huge bump on his forehead. He looked like he had been beaten up. His boss asked, "What happened?" The man, still a little dazed, said, "It was terrible, just terrible. I was leaving my house this morning and fell down the entire flight of stairs." His boss replied, "And this took an hour?"*

It's been said that we only use 10% of our brains in reaching our potential, and although that has never been proven, when we become impatient I believe we only use 10% of our hearts. If you communicate 100% understanding, 100% of the time, your child will trust you 100% of the time. If you communicate 40% understanding most of the time, then your child will trust you 40% of the time, and so on.

Want more proof of the critical long term impact of being emotionally understood? In 2017 the result of a landmark 75-year Harvard Study of Adult Development, found one conclusion that surpasses all others in what determines true happiness.

> *"It is not what you do or who you are. It is how emotionally honest you are with another in close relationships; it is the extent to which you can relax and be seen for who you truly are, and truly see another."* This is hugely significant because while it's important to

be who we are, we can still remain unhappy when our special qualities remain invisible to those whom we want to be seen by."

SLOW DOWN

Rule One is not about fixing anything. It's about being in the moment and calibrating the level of emotional and or physical experience your child is having so you will know how to respond. The secret is calibration. Before you can communicate understanding, you have to listen for understanding. We never know when a moment becomes a memory.

"Listen to me!" That's what everyone says when they want you to know something important. "Listen to me!" What they really mean is, "Read between the lines and find the hidden meaning." Calibrate their level of emotional upset so that when it comes time to reflect it back, it matches exactly the way they are feeling! They are also saying please understand *all* of what I'm saying, not just a part of it. The operative word is *all*. Don't be holding or looking at your phone, and if the TV is on in the same room, turn it off. You don't have to be perfect, but you do have to be present. In effect you want to be saying:

"If it's important to you, it's everything to me." When we don't know how to master a moment, we can't master a relationship.

As parents we have an enormous amount of information to teach every day to guide behavior. But sometimes we should delay the teaching until we have successfully communicated back what a child is feeling, thinking or saying. When you delay your teaching for a few minutes, you reset the conditions for a different outcome. That's when children will be open to consider another point of view or other choices. Too

Before you can communicate understanding, you have to listen for understanding

often parents try to fix the moment, without first acknowledging the moment in a natural way.

A teenager or middle-schooler who may say in a big fit of raging anger, *"I wish I had a different father,"* should be met with heartfelt belief, no matter how painful it is to hear. *"Dina, you are boiling mad at me. A part of you wishes I wasn't your father right now. This is not working out the way you want. You are not at all happy that I won't let you go with your friends."*

When she says, *"Yeah, I'm not at all happy and I won't ever be!"*

Tell her, *"I believe you. Still, no matter how angry you are at me now, my love for you never changes."*

Show you accept her feelings without debate, rather than, *"I know you don't mean that." There is a huge difference between accepting a child's feelings and accepting his or her behavior.* Bad feelings are always tolerated; bad behavior is not. Liquidating those feelings reduces tension.

One dramatic way to help listen for understanding is to change your focus. Instead of listening to their story in your head, try listening to their story with your heart. It will lead to a dramatically different outcome. Difficult feelings are painful to feel and hard to express.

"Julie, you have no good clothes. It's embarrassing to go to school looking uncool. You're tired of wearing hand-me-downs from your sister. These clothes make you feel bad about yourself."

The takeaway: Slowdown, otherwise it leads to kept secrets, detached feelings and harbored resentment. You can't rush emotional conversations.

LET'S DO A QUICK CHECK NOW

Let's use our relationship in this moment (you, the reader, with me), to practice what you think I'm trying to communicate so far. Remember, you don't have to agree with a single word I'm saying. You do, however, have to express that you take me seriously and you believe that I really believe what

I'm saying. After calibrating what level my intensity is on, your summary might sound something like this:

> When we don't know how to master a moment, we can't master a relationship

"Wow, Brenner! You believe the missing link in close relationships is knowing how to express consistent empathy and caring. You believe if everyone knew how to express understanding in a very deep way, relationships would be transformed. It doesn't matter how young or how old we are. No fake listening, no faking caring. No fake anything. You actually believe that showing a deep understanding is much more satisfying than even being loved. I know I've left out some of your important quotes and a lot more detail, but would you say I completely get the essence of what you communicated to me?"

As the author, I would say this in response to you:

"Holy smokes! Wow! You just blew me away. You got it all! I really believe you when you say, you could add even more! I trust you so much more." Well, we just experienced being in sync with each other and you didn't have to agree with a single word I said. And—it all took less than 30-seconds.

BE THE HEAD COACH

Raising a family is very much like coaching a thriving sports team, which is why great parenting can be compared to great coaching. All great coaches know how to bring out the best in team unity, respect, personal responsibility and achievement. Being the head coach of a family means consistently being responsible for modeling and maintaining the integrity of these core values. While most parents would agree with those values, they differ on how to communicate them. This sports metaphor is not meant to change the parents personality, but to give a simple yet bold image to mirror those qualities. Parents report that this shift in mindset to lead as the head coach of your family eases their anxieties during times of conflict. The only caveat to this metaphor is that unlike sports where emotions run high, here, parents remain elegant with a calming tone of voice.

OUR MELODY

As you put *Rule One* into action, there's one thing to keep in mind above everything else: Although our words are super important, they are not nearly as important as our tone of voice, facial expressions and body language. I call this collection of physical expressions, *'Our Melody.'* No one wants to listen or cooperate when we look or sound arrogant, negative, a know-it-all, sarcastic, singsongy, too loud or controlling.

> You can feel a look more powerfully than words

Our melody decisively determines how other people feel about us and the level of trust we project. It remains the single most important influence in how we relate to one another. It doesn't matter how nice our words are, *90% of our real message is in our melody!* You can feel a look more powerfully than words.

Think of your tone of voice, facial expressions and body language as smooth jazz: easy on the ears and heart. The 17th-century philosopher Voltaire had it right when he said, *"The road to the heart are the ears."* This doesn't mean that our words don't matter or we can't raise our voices, show anger or upset. Sure we can. However, we must always control o*ur melody* if we *want* to build trust, excite understanding and project respect.

I repeat this vital insight with each rule, so we never forget that while our words are important, *'Our Melody'* really is everything!

Rule One

CAN EMPATHY BE TAUGHT

The short answer is yes. Empathy is a skill. We can see the level of empathy some kids have early on in the way they help around the house, enjoy babysitting, or care for others who are not feeling well. They are rich in their capacity to nurture and already have an awareness of how they affect others. The opposite can also be true. Some kids (like some adults), are preoccupied with themselves and struggle in showing others that they care. The 11th century Rabbi and poet, Moshe Ibn Ezra would say, "Words that come from the heart, enter the heart."

> Although empathy can be learned, it can't be forced!

Isn't it interesting that we can travel 240,000 miles to walk on the moon, but sometimes find it too difficult to walk in someone else's shoes. Yet, the greatest distance we will ever travel is the distance from our head to our heart. Although empathy can be learned, it can't be forced! Instead of telling a child to apologize after fighting with a sibling, it is better to first inquire with a caring tone, "How do you think Robert is feeling now? What might you do to help him feel better?" As our five-and six-year-olds become more aware of themselves, they will also become more aware of others.

"Michael, can you feel the big smile you have on your face? I can see you're feeling happy."

Or, *"Laura, when you yell, it makes you feel tired and angry. Let's talk it through calmly so you can tell me what you want me to know."*

There are multiple ways we can teach empathy. The first of course is through modeling the natural caring between parent and child. *The second way we develop empathy is through learned self-awareness (Rule Three).* The more we help a child discover how they feel emotionally and physically, the more they will be able to recognize those same feelings in others. Children, (like some adults) are often sometimes unaware how they feel.

They are not yet in touch with their bodies. The more you help your child make those connections, the quicker they will learn to identify them.

Other ways to teach empathy include:

1. *Discuss other people's feelings.*
2. *Allow your child to see you vulnerable without being overly needy.*
3. *Give names for feelings.*
4. *Practice making faces that reflect different emotions.*
5. *Never deny your child's feelings.*
6. *Express your own feelings when appropriate.*
7. *Sometimes, ask about your child's feelings hypothetically.*
8. *Show empathy towards strangers.*

EMPATHY VS. SYMPATHY

Most people think sympathy and empathy are interchangeable. They are vastly different. When we communicate sympathy, the relationship is usually more distant. The feeling is felt as, "It happened to you, not me." We use expressions like, "I feel terrible for you." "That's so sad." "That's awful." "I am so sorry."

> Most people think sympathy and empathy are interchangeable. They are vastly different

Sympathy sends a pity and sorrow message that feeds the narrative that the person is a victim and is weak. In close relationships, we never want to communicate sympathy. Never! Showing sympathy can also include giving premature advice. Such advice (before it is asked for), is often taken as a lack of confidence in the other person to figure it out for him/herself. It also carries an additional risk; if the advice doesn't fit, you will not be seen as trustworthy or wise.

Empathy on the other hand, allows us to anticipate how others want us to respond with a quiet feeling that says, "I will travel with you on your terms, to see what you see. I will stay with you as long as it takes," all without trying to fix anything or give advice. Properly expressed, empathy also carries a powerful non-verbal message, "You have the strength to defeat your situation!" *(See Rule Five)*

"Emily, I see it all in your eyes. It's a bad feeling to be around your friend Shelly at school. Sometimes you wish she wasn't at your school so it could be your turn to be popular, then the kids would like you just as much. You wish tomorrow there was no school."

EXAMPLES OF EMPATHY

"Anyone would feel the same way."

"You're scared to go, and you're excited to go."

"Sometimes you wish you didn't have a sister."

"Part of you wants to tell me, and part of you doesn't."

"I love seeing the excitement and exhilaration on your face."

"I can feel how uncomfortable it was for you to watch him do that!"

"It's easy to understand why you want to stay in bed the whole day."

In the neurology literature which deals with the analysis of the nervous system, Dr. Paul Ekman, a leading world expert on emotions, classifies "empathy" into three different categories:

(1) *Cognitive Empathy:* intellectually knowing what another person is feeling.

(2) *Emotional Empathy*: feeling what another person is feeling.

(3) *Compassionate Empathy*: knowing how to respond to another person in the way they want.

> It's not enough to think you understand, or to feel what others feel. You must prove it, by showing it

The highest level of empathy is of course, *compassionate empathy*. It's not enough to think you understand, or to feel what others feel. You must prove it, by showing it. That's why we sometimes find ourselves turning-away from a kind-hearted person. *It's not enough just to be kind-hearted. You have to know exactly what to say and what to do in order to satisfy the heart of another.* The wrong question at the wrong time, giving premature advice, a well-intentioned hug, a missed timed cry-along, or a quiet blank stare, can all be a big turn-off.

A great example of knowing what to say and do comes from Wayne Bryan, the wise father of twin sons who became the most successful tennis doubles champions in U.S. history. He offers this advice to parents whose children play sports and experience feeling down after playing poorly or losing a game. Depending on the age, and as you walk to the car, there are only a few things to say:

Gatorade or water?

Where do you want to eat?

Do you want to drive home or do you want me to?

You can feel the wisdom of holding back the small talk to fill that awkward silence. There is no advice-giving, no fixing, no pep talk, no more questions. Just the caring sound of silence until a more natural moment opens up. Emotional conversations cannot be rushed. By allowing your children more time to express themselves, you allow more time for them to get in touch with their true feelings, as well as fashion their own plan of action.

Here's my own mantra: *Before I tell you what I think, it is more important I learn what you think.* This also allows children to get rid of their bad feelings in order to make room for problem-solving, growth and cooperation. When we understand the "why" behind behavior, the "what to do" and "what to say" become more obvious.

"Michael, sometimes it's hard to put into words the way we feel. Take your time."

It helps to remember not to try to immediately fix what is wrong in the moment. Besides, you rarely can. Let your child see and feel that you *do not* experience them as difficult, even though in that moment they are. As a practicing therapist, I do not believe in psychological cures in the same way we can cure a stomach ache or the measles. Rather, when we know how to emotionally respond in the moment, the real meaning of a cure becomes self-evident and lasting.

FAKE EMPATHY

When parents first learn the power of expressive empathy, they have a tendency to over-do it. Resist using expressions such as, —*"I see," "It sounds like," "It looks like," "It might be."* Children, like any adult, can spot phony empathy a mile away. *"I see you're frustrated!" "I see you don't want to go." "It sounds like you're upset." "I see you want to stay."* Very quickly the whole conversation starts to sound like a Jackie Mason routine.

These types of expressions may seem like a safe way to appear caring, but in reality they create distance, as though you're only an observer. You will sound out of touch and appear robotic. Such expressions are superficial. You don't want to sound like a therapist, especially a bad one. Parents can talk too much and need to know that not every moment needs to be spent on providing a life lesson, fixing a bad attitude or delivering a science lecture.

One way to help us slow down and connect is to use *big little words:* "Oh" and "Mmm." These little words said with care can show genuine interest. Saying, "Oh" and "Mmm" helps us say less rather than leaping in with premature advice or opinions. They also give the child more time and opportunity to solve his or her problem.

EMPATHY INCLUDES POSITIVE EMOTIONS TOO

When we think about empathy, we think mostly in terms of negative and sad emotions. In truth, empathy equally combines our positive emotions too, such as curiosity, pride, joy, gratitude, optimism, enthusiasm or even laughter.

These wonderful positive emotions can be found in moments that include a twinkle in your child's eye when they discover something familiar, a curious smile exploring their own backyard, or maybe it's simply the feeling of comfort after a hot bath and being covered in toasty towels. Rather than express those smaller positive emotions and experiences, a parent may launch into 20 questions, "Sam what do you see?" "Did you like your bath, Jeffrey?" "Was it good?" or, ignore those moments completely, all while waiting for bigger moments to arrive.

Let's contrast those responses with positive descriptive empathizing:

"Look how good you feel, Jeffrey, being all toasty and warm. Your face and body are so relaxed. You're in a cloud of comfort."

Or, after reading a fun book aloud, you turn to your son and say, *"Michael, I love the curiosity on your face. I can see the wheels turning in your mind. Let's look it up later and see what we can find."*

To help in this process and increase your child's self-awareness, watch their faces for cues and reflect back what you see. *"Emily, I love the care in your smile when you play with your American Girl Doll.™ You have a lot of love in your heart for her."* When we're young, we begin to find out, in part, who we are through others.

With children we want to be colorful and effusive, reflecting how they feel as well as how they make us feel. Combining the positive ways your child feels along with your own feelings, will draw you both closer.

"Andy, I'm loving the excitement on your face. I'm getting happy all over just looking at you."

" You make me smile from ear to ear. My heart is so full when we laugh together."

"Lori, I am floating on air after hearing that news. My heart just grew to the moon."

"Jackson, I can see by the expression on your face you are feeling so proud that you made the soccer team. Now I'm beaming too just from looking at your beautiful face."

"I think about you all the time when we're not together."

"I love when our eyes connect. I feel so close to you."

Some people are stingy with expressing positive emotions, in the way some people are stingy with their money. They hold on tight to every penny, the way they hold on tight to every positive word. They may have generous hearts, but they do not have generous emotional ways. Often they are unaware of how they come across. When we become more generous with our positive emotions we also experience improved health.

FEELING FEELINGS IN OUR BODY

At the Institute of Heart Math (www.heartmath.org), researchers have come across a stunning finding regarding our emotions and our bodies: The heart muscle is physically responsive to emotional input. With each beat, there are emotional messages that influence our physical well-being. Our brain takes just 100 milliseconds to detect and process the smallest change in the human face and just 300 milliseconds to mirror this change in our own bodies. You can see this, for example, when someone blushes or when our eyes well up with tears, or the heart beats faster from excitement, tension or fear. It also helps to explain why, when we feel deeply hurt or moved, we sometimes say, "I'm heart-broken" or "You've touched my heart."

As a result when we deliver or receive any emotionally charged message, positive or negative, there is a generated physiological effect on the body. Tension and stress gives us a knot in our stomachs or a "lump in our throat." Overwhelming joy can make us feel choked up, and anticipatory excitement generates "butterflies in our gut." These physiological responses to emotional situations explain why, when we say we have a "change of heart," it leads to a change in behavior. When your teenager tells you that a certain aunt or uncle makes her feel sick to her stomach every time she sees him or her, you may hear it as, "He makes me uncomfortable." However, many times that physical expression is meant literally, in the same way when you sometimes say certain people make you tense. When we are deeply in tune with another, we can actually experience a fleeting portion of that physical feeling. That is what we mean when we say, when you 'hear' certain words, you should 'feel' them. The value of emotions comes from sharing them, and not just having them.

"Alex, when Uncle Teddy comes over I will make sure he does not pick you up in the air the way he always does, or asks so many questions. I know he upsets you. Let's stay close together till he leaves."

Think about it this way: You know that feeling you get when you eat something spoiled and you become nauseous? Just seeing that same food in the refrigerator, or even getting a small whiff of that scent can make you sick all over again. Well, that's what our reaction should be when we hear how others feel. We need to feel a little nauseous too so we respond in the

> Healthy feelings are like an alarm clock that automatically goes off at just the right time

Rule One

right way. We're not rushing into the arms of others when we are met with flat emotions and mechanical gestures of caring.

What makes feeling someone else's feelings so important is that you never have to be reminded that the other person is waiting for a certain response. Healthy feelings are like an alarm clock that automatically goes off at just the right time. If your feelings are shut down, your alarm won't go off. When someone tells you, "Sorry, I forgot again to respond in the right way, in all likelihood the reason is not because they didn't remember, it's because they didn't feel. Too many adults get uncomfortable with their feelings because they don't know what to do with them, so they learn to do away with them. The problem is when they need their feelings or instincts, they can't find them. When this becomes a pattern, professional help is needed.

In the classic movie, Winnie the Pooh, Piglet helps us to better understand this emotional life-skill when he asks: "How do you spell 'love'?" Pooh replies, "You don't spell it...you feel it."

> The deciding factor if someone is emotionally healthy is determined by how well they are in control of their thoughts, feelings and behaviors

WHAT IS EMOTIONAL INTELLIGENCE

> We experience those with emotional health as calm, patient and trustworthy

Emotional intelligence is the ability to understand and regulate one's own emotions while simultaneously knowing how to read and respond to another person's emotions. The deciding factor if someone is emotionally healthy is determined by how well they are in control of their thoughts, feelings and behaviors. Just because we feel something, doesn't mean it's true or we should act on them.

We must examine those feelings first. As a result, we know **when** to communicate, **what** to communicate and **how** to communicate. This is why those who have emotional intelligence and self-control are generally happier in life.

We experience those with emotional health as calm, patient and trustworthy. They seem natural in their own skin and make others feel comfortable around them. They never act defensive or have to prove they're right when conflict arises. You don't leave their company with that after-feeling of, "Boy, I'm glad they're finally gone, I'm drained from their emotional games." Ironically, those who perpetually hide behind their own false masks and defensiveness, drain themselves.

The greater our ability to control ourselves, the higher our emotional intelligence. The good news is that while IQ seems to be fixed, we can increase our EQ (Emotional Intelligence) substantially.

HOW TO SHOW A COMPLETE UNDERSTANDING

COLLECT THE INFORMATION

Listen with your eyes. Collecting information in the moment is not a two-way debate in which you offer your point of view. Wisdom begins first with silence. Your goal is to help your children tell their story. Like an acoustical soundboard, absorb what you see and hear *before* bouncing it back. This can take as little as 10 seconds to 3 minutes. Here's how to connect:

a. **Don't fake listen.** "Take your time, I want to hear everything you have to say," and mean it! Listen to their face.
   - Don't deny, invalidate or minimize what your child is saying.

- Don't interrupt; wait for a natural break.
- Don't give advice.
- Don't correct.
- Don't change the subject.
- Don't lecture, debate or over-talk.

b. **Keep yourself in check; your child is watching.** We remember 15% of what we hear and 85% of what we see! Control your facial expressions, body language and tone of voice. If your child is communicating something serious, don't laugh or smile. Look serious. Nothing is funny. As you listen for understanding, don't look confused or disappointed. No twisted faces. Keep your tone of voice warm and caring. When you smile, smile slowly; it will create the feeling of more warmth and connection. Do not be loud.

c. **Rock your head slowly up and down with sensitivity.**

d. **Maintain eye contact in a natural way.** This conveys, "What you are saying is important. You are important." People who avert their gaze are often seen as untrustworthy.

e. **Lean slightly forward with interest.**

f. **With a caring tone of voice use short observational expressions.** *"Mmmm." "I see." "Yes, that is difficult." "Wow!" "What a dilemma you're in."*

g. **Limit your questions.** Too many questions signal you are completely clueless!

h. **Refrain from too many "why" questions.** To children and teenagers, the question "Why?" is often taken as disapproval and displeasure. Even a simple, "Why did you do that?" will evoke the memoy and the feelings of, "Why in the world did you ever do something as stupid as that?"

i. **Show emotional interest.**
   "Tell me more."
   "What's in your heart that you want me to know?"

CALIBRATE

a. While you are collecting the information, mentally assign in your mind on a scale of zero to 10, what level of emotional and/or physical experience your child or teenager is having. In other words, to what degree of upset or excitement is he or she experiencing? Is it mild, neutral or over-the-top? Do not minimize, dismiss or exaggerate what you see or hear. We do this so when it comes times to reflect back their feelings, you will be prepared to match their experience exactly with depth and accuracy. This takes only seconds.

SUMMARIZE BACK IN YOUR OWN WORDS IN DETAIL

a. **Using your own words, but with the same meaning, tell their story back with 100% accuracy and detail.** If there's an emotional history, don't forget to include that too. Think in terms of one headline that says it all, and lead with that. *Your tone of voice must convey you believe them in every way.* Think of your voice as a matching melody. Validate their experience using original dramatic and graphic language, and not just repeating back their same words, or simplistically saying, "I understand" or, "I hear you." *When we have emotional connection, no amount of detail is too much. When we don't have connection, any detail is too much.*

    Imagine reading a paragraph in a book and someone asks, "What did the author say?" You repeat back the paragraph word for word. You prove you have a good memory, but not a good understanding. Speak about it in detail. Remember, your children are not really looking for agreement, they're looking to be believed! To do that, you must say it in the exact way they want to hear it and not in the way you feel like saying it. Keep it tight, but leave nothing important out. Be exceedingly accurate, don't exaggerate or minimize. Typically, an empathic summary can take anywhere from 10 seconds to two minutes. It should match exactly what their feelings were.

"Sandra, it has become very clear that you hate your high school, and you're so tired of all the fighting at home too. For a long time you have been convinced I have no understanding of you, your tastes in music, friends, clothes... everything really! Even my talking to you now is too much, and is a turn-off. The truth is I finally can see what you have seen all along in myself."

"Allison, you don't like me right now for making you leave the toy store. You're furious at me now. You want to stay and play more with those trains. You want me to leave you alone until you are ready to go."

"Jacob, at this moment you wish you had a different brother. You are filled with resentment for him. He seems to get all the attention and all the good stuff. I can see you are tired of putting up with this. The whole situation is unfair. You've been feeling this way a long time, and you want me to do something about it, starting now!"

b. **Keep your melody in tune.** Be sure your tone of voice, as well as your body language, facial expressions and vocabulary are *all calibrated* to match how your child or teenager is feeling. Maintain relaxed warm eye contact.

c. **Use the right emotional vocabulary.** Typically, children with behavioral issues do not know how to interpret their own emotional experiences. If we narrate their experiences, they can make the right connections. *"Roberta, you have a furious (puzzled, exuberant) look on your face now. I can see you're upset. You are not happy!"* By naming the specific emotion (see the list below) and matching it to their experience, your child will become better at identifying and expressing how he or she feels.

Children who have better emotional vocabularies often show less aggression when anger or frustration arrives suddenly. They know how and when to put feelings into words, not actions. They have fewer episodes of acting out because they have language. In other words, instead of using their hands, they use their words. Parents can also model this behavior when they describe their own feelings. "Wow, what an exhausting day I had today. I was speaking to a business friend who infuriates me. He is so stubborn. I feel annoyed each time I talk with him."

Or, you might tell your eight-year-old, *"Alan, my heart grows so big when I see how relaxed you can be with your younger brother." "Laura, when I come home from work and see your face, I feel like I'm floating three feet off the ground."*

It's not easy speaking in colorful emotional language if we are not used to it. It is the reason so many of us look for pre-written greeting cards to express just the right sentiment. We should go way beyond using the same basic seven emotions to express ourselves: happiness, sadness, fear, anger, surprise, contempt and disgust. To enhance your child's emotional vocabulary, teach new emotional words everyday.

Here's a small handful of the hundreds of emotional words we can inject everyday into our conversations to help children learn how they feel and or, how we feel.

AGITATED	DISTRESSED	SCARED
ALARMED	DELIGHTED	SECURE
UPSET	DISTURBED	SENSITIVE
ANXIOUS	EAGER	SHAKY
AWKWARD	EMBARRASSED	SHOCKED
CAUTIOUS	ENCOURAGED	SHY
COMFORTABLE	ENRAGED	SUSPICIOUS
CHEERFUL	ENTHUSED	STRESSED
DISAPPOINTED	EXASPERATED	SLEEPY
DISCOURAGED	SAD	SILLY
DISGUSTED	SAFE	

Rule One

CONFIRM

Now that you've finished expressing a complete understanding, get the confirmation. Here are the two steps to do that.

a. Look for confirmation on your child's face that says: "Yes, I can see you know what I'm thinking and feeling." When you see that signal, maintain eye contact with a knowing nod that says: "Yep, I get it." Don't just say you understand. Show it on your face.

b. If you feel your child doesn't think you have the full picture, ask with concern, "Do I have it all?" "Am I missing something?" "I really want to understand everything." Stay calm and relaxed. Wait for the answer and continue again to repeat back in your own words the new information. Look again for confirmation. If there is again new information, repeat steps two and three. Calibrate and summarize back in your own words. Take as many rounds as necessary.

ALWAYS PUT THE RELATIONSHIP ABOVE THE SITUATION

Rarely are acting-out behaviors the real problem. When mom found out that her 14-year-old daughter Michelle was still hanging around a girl at school who was also a bad influence, her first impulse was to say: "Michelle, you promised me you were done with Katie. Why did you lie to me?" Instead, she paused and put the relationship above the lying.

"It must have been so hard to keep this secret for so long without telling me. I am sorry I lost your trust. Let's talk about what's happening between us that you did not want me to know."

Mom's empathetic response shows that she values the relationship above everything else! It creates the subtext: Nothing is more important than you and me. Nothing! After all, if the relationship is strained she will have little influence over Michelle anyway. It is impossible to gain emotional trust without showing empathy.

A father who sees his son struggling to start his homework might say:

"Jeffrey, I wish it was the weekend so you had no homework. School can be tiring and right now you don't have the energy to start your math homework. You want it all to go away. Me too."

Talking this way allows you to connect before you correct. Allowing a few moments to pass can make all the difference in the world. Then you can say, *"Maybe in fifteen minutes you'll feel like starting it. Then again, maybe you won't. Let's knock it out now so you'll have more time to do other things you like."*

Too often parents tend to focus on what the child is saying or doing, rather than on what he is experiencing internally. In no way am I suggesting that we should elevate feelings above our behaviors. Not at all. We must hold our children, as well as ourselves, to be responsible for our actions. What I am saying *is* that *when we consistently bypass feelings, it will lead to disturbed behavior.*

Healthy parent-child relationships are relational, not transactional. They are concerned with what is behind the behavior. The prize is the process of 'how and why' of what is being expressed in contrast to primarily focusing on the facts of what is being said. They are also acutely aware of their 'own melody' when they respond.

"Janice, how do you feel about continuing your friendship with Marci?"

"How are you experiencing our talk right now?"

"You look like you are having some reaction to what I am saying."

"Michael, you want more respect from me even though you are resisting what I am saying."

"What is it about the way I am talking now that don't you like?"

"What is it about this subject you like?

YES, BRING UP THE PAST
- THE ELEPHANT IN THE ROOM

In addition to knowing how to acknowledge what is happening in the moment, we must also know how to acknowledge and express was has happened in the past, especially if a relationship is in need of repair or a reset. The elephant in the room is something we have all experienced. Whether it was a silly fight that was never really resolved, a trauma, or a consistent pattern of emotional neglect, the challenge becomes knowing how to bring up past hurts. Often when this happens, we walk on eggshells in order to avoid making things worse. Most parents are so relieved it is already in the past and even more relieved to leave it there. The problem with this pattern is that it makes the person who is hurting want to give up on the relationship.

To help us get through those roadblocks and give voice to 'the elephant in the room,' we must put aside our discomfort, ego and vulnerability in order to communicate past hurts. As literary award winner and author John Green so poignantly reminds us, *"That's the thing about pain, it demands to be felt."*

"Kim, even though you haven't said anything to me in days about my not going to your basketball game, I know I let you down. The truth is I can be selfish. I'm always making excuses. I've hurt you too many times. I'm going to change my ways, and I ask you for your forgiveness."

"David, we had a rough time yesterday shopping for a new backpack. I can still feel your anger at me for not allowing you to get the one you wanted. Would you be okay if we talked about it some more together? I would like to hear more about what you have to say."

Parents must remember not to protect their own ego or reputation when they are looking to establish emotional trust. When we model vulnerability, we set the conditions for our kids to see first hand the power of self-examination.

A mother of four came to realize that for years she has shown favoritism to her oldest son. After becoming aware of this, she decided to confront this truth head-on. The mom found a quiet place to talk where she knew there would be no distraction. She began by saying,

"Alan, I have a confession to make. May I tell you about it?" After hearing 'Yes', she continued. *"My heart is heavy because I have hurt you so much by spending so much time with your brother, Steven.*

I have ignored your needs and your heart. I haven't been there for you in the same ways I have been there for Steven. I can feel how much resentment you have for me. I have created feelings of jealousy in you. I hope in time you can forgive me. I am going to spend a lot more time with you from now on. This will never happen again! Is it okay that I tell you all this?"

If you see your child is getting fatigued from this emotional moment, you might add, *"Let's continue talking about this later when you have more energy."* If they indicate they want to continue, then dive deep into more truth. This process is not a one-time event where our emotional history is forgiven in that moment. On the contrary, we must prove our way back each day.

To help make that happen, I recommend bringing up past hurts from time to time, so that your child or teenager believes that you are still bothered by what you have done and your 'new self-discovery' is indeed for real.

"Jessica, since our talk last month, I'm so glad I came to know the truth about my moods and what I've done to you in the past. I know I keep telling you, but I am so happy I finally see what you see." In time your child will tell you, *"Mom it's okay now, you don't have to keep telling me. I believe you."*

CONSTANT QUESTIONS ARE NOT CONVERSATIONS

For many parents, asking a lot of questions seems like a surefire way of showing care and interest. Lots of questions are good when you are interviewing a vendor or employee, but not when you're in a close relationship. You don't want to be seen as an interrogator. It communicates, "I'm not up to speed on your life. I don't know your likes, your dislikes, or your history." You will appear clueless and more transactional.

> Constant questions also carry the risk of coming off more curious than caring

Constant questions also carry the risk of coming off more curious than caring. When did it start? How long has it been going on? What did it feel like? When relationships drift, constant questions make it worse. They even create the desire to lie a little, or be extra brief in order to keep a safe emotional distance. One father who had an argument in the afternoon with his teenage son but still hadn't resolved it by evening, asked him: *"What's bothering you?"* That question ignored their earlier argument and sparked even more distance. *If there is understanding, you have everything! If there is no understanding, there's only a bottomless pit of questions.* It is why in Chassidic teachings, it is said: a wise parent is someone who can see the unshed tear and hear the unasked question.

A mother with three teenage daughters found one of them in the bathroom visibly upset. She asked: *"Are you okay?"* Clearly the mother could have seen things were not okay before asking that question. Later her daughter said: *"Mom, it bothers me that you never read my feelings. You ask me too many questions, and I feel you don't know me. I also don't like that you are always offering me advice that never fits."*

A two-year-old playing with a piece of cardboard doesn't need to be asked: *"Jonathan, what is that you have in your hand? What are you going do with it? And look, Jonathan, it can bend... blah blah blah, blah."* We already know he doesn't know what it's called. If he could talk the way he feels, he might say, *"Ma, stop with the questions! I'm just playing. Let me be. I don't care if it bends. I'm just trying to eat it!"*

Mornings for some parents have a tendency to follow the

same pattern of inquiry. They wake their children up with a fresh brew of questions: How did you sleep last night? How do you feel? Are you hungry? Everything... is a question!! Instead, let a little time pass. If something is wrong, you will soon know it or see it. Better to softly say: *"Good morning, sweetheart"* and watch for the cues.

The same goes for asking, *"What do you want for breakfast?"* When we're in tune with those we care for, we should know their preferences. Even certain questions about going food shopping can become irritating. *"I'm going to the market now, what kind of cereal do you want?"* Your teen is likely to think, *"Mom, don't you know what I like by now?"*

INSTEAD OF QUESTIONS

One suggestion that encourages children to open up about their day is to avoid the most common checklist question of all time, *"How was school today?"* Instead, make this caring statement, *"Sam, tell me about your day."* The question, *"How was school today?"* can create feelings of tension. The statement, *"Tell me about your day"* is a far more relaxed way to start talking. It allows you to say things in any order you like. Your child won't feel like there are right and wrong answers. When he or she begins to open-up, you might add,

"Tell me more." As a parent which would you prefer to hear? *"What did you do today?"* Or, *"Tell me about your day!"*

At the same time, when you do need to ask a question, try to be specific, such as: *"What was the lesson today in science class?"* or *"What was it like when...?"* Such questions inspire discussion and lead to more spontaneous detail.

Another effective way to limit direct questions is with statements that begin with, *"I was wondering?" "I was wondering if you still wanted be friends with Alex now that you know he is not loyal?"*

"I was wondering if you're still upset with your brother because he wouldn't go outside with you this afternoon?" Or,

Rule One

"Steven, I remember we were talking about your teacher and how he embarrassed you in class last week. I was wondering if he did that again today?"

"I wonder" statements also encourage raw emotions and ideas to be expressed spontaneously without feeling judged. Other strategies to limit asking direct questions is to make observational comments.

"Samantha, I noticed when you came home you had sadness on your face." Or, "David, it's obvious something happened today. Why don't you unwind and we can talk about what happened later."

We also want to be on the look-out for "Why?"questions. If our tone of voice is not humble and caring, the question "Why?" can be taken the wrong way. It can come across as disapproval and displeasure. Even a simple, *"Why did you do that?"* will likely evoke early memories and the feelings of, *"Why in the world did you ever do something as stupid as that?"*

The question can also lead a child to give an answer which includes, "I don't know" (making the child again feel dumb), or it may force him to lie or make up an answer that he thinks his parent (or teacher) wants to hear. Better to say: "Tell me more," allowing the child to come to a more natural way of revealing the truth.

TRANSACTIONAL PARENTS

"Did you do what I asked?" "How was your day?" "Did you remember to bring it?"

Transactional parents' constant questions, severely limits their ability to connect emotionally and build trust. They think in outcomes. They are more concerned with facts, goals and results rather than focusing on the underlying psychological process, feelings and motivations. Transactional parents are also known as checklist parents. They look at everything in concrete terms, in order to advance an agenda. They lack empathy and insight.

One father texted his daughter without considering what

> Transactional parents are also known as checklist parents. They look at everything in concrete terms, in order to advance an agenda. They lack empathy and insight

her experience was in the moment, *"What time will you be home?"* His critical tone of voice conveys his lack of caring. A better way of getting his question answered would have been to acknowledge first what his child was experiencing at the time:

"Kate, I hope you're having fun, I know you haven't forgot to be home at 4:30."

Transactional parents have little patience for behavior nuance. They value information over relationships, unwittingly making their children feel anxious and inferior. Everything is a question. Although their caring comes from their heart, it always feels like it comes with a price and wanting something back. Some parents confuse making sandwiches, keeping schedules and staying organized with relationship skills. As a consequence of their rigidity, children pull away emotionally and lose their desire to reveal their secrets and truest feelings.

Transactional parents are often so uncomfortable with their own emotions, that they come to believe that it is best for their children to get over their own negative emotions quickly and suck it up. They believe that distracting a child from negative feelings has long term positive benefits and will make them stronger. They do not view negative emotions as an opportunity for intimacy.

Denying a child's feelings, runs the risk that one day their children will no longer be able to identify how they are feeling. After so many years of repression, how will they know how to ask for help? How will they know when they are hurting emotionally? Who will know?

When I give my *Parenting Without Therapy*™ workshops, I like to tell this light-hearted story:

Rule One

One night a wife found her husband standing over their baby's crib. Silently she watched him. As he stood looking down at the sleeping infant, she saw on his face a mixture of emotions: amazement, enchantment, delight, even a little doubt. Touched by his unusual display of emotions, she snuggled up next to her husband saying: "A penny for your thoughts, sweetheart?" His reply: "It's amazing! I just can't see how anybody can make a crib like that for only $99.00."

It goes without saying that transactional parents have the same deep love for their children as all parents. The good news is that those parents who reflect this kind of parenting style now have a proven playbook for a new *Reset*.

DON'T LOSE YOUR SENSE OF HUMOR

We don't need to go to the Mayo Clinic to know that laughter can often be the best medicine. The problem is, too many parents take themselves too seriously and have forgotten how to be light- hearted with their children, especially their teenagers. Parents are so caught up in trying to get their children to do what they want or teach them some big lesson, they lose their sense of humor. Too often parents forget that the shortest distance between two people can be a light-hearted talk and a good laugh. Observational studies indicate that parents of the most socially competent children laugh and smile more often

When sixteen-year-old David told his father he wanted to quit school, his father said, *"David, let's go out, get a burger and talk about it."* Turns out it wasn't so much school, as it was getting his driver's license and wanting more independence. The trick is to read your child's mood and see if the timing is right for a little humor to reduce the tension. If the timing is right , then look for what's funny in the situation. *"I'll tell you David, I'd rather see you find a wife before you leave school."*

Rule Two

TALK WITH RESPECT

SELF-WORTH

*Children learn more from what you are,
than what you teach.*
—W.E.B. DU BOIS

A physician was once asked, "What is the best medicine for boosting self-worth in a child?"

Without missing a beat he said, "Show respect."

The patient asked, "What happens if it doesn't work?"

The physician replied, "Increase the dose!"

Now that we understand why *Rule One* is the foundation for building empathy, let's take a closer look at why *Rule Two* is the foundation for building self-worth. Talking with respect is much more than talking nice or staying calm. If I had to describe in a single idea what it means to talk with respect, it would be consistently making the other person feel looked up

> If I had to describe in a single idea what it means to talk with respect, it would be consistently making the other person feel looked up to, admired and with status, especially during times of conflict

> **There is a huge difference between feeling loved and feeling respected**

to, admired and with status, especially during times of conflict. No moodiness, sarcasm or impatience. Speaking with respect always has a gracious and elegant tone about it.

The need to feel respected runs very deep. Without it, we threaten self-worth and increase risky and rebellious behavior. Think of yourself as the 'head coach' leading your child by example. It will keep you humble and focused. It has long been believed that to imbue self-worth in children, we simply just have to love them. In part that's true; however, no matter how much we love them, it will never replace the underlying feelings of not measuring up to those whose respect we craved, but never received. There is a huge difference between feeling loved and feeling respected.

When parents are asked if they talk with respect, many often reflexively say, *"Of course, I do."* However, parents should ask themselves: Do I bark orders? Do I interrupt and come across like a know-it-all? Do I sing my words in a childish way to sound sappy sweet? Do I continually lecture? Does my face look tense? Am I always in a hurry? Am I sarcastic?

What makes talking with respect so critical is that those who have an inner feeling of worthiness, also believe they are worthy of being loved. It breaks my heart to know that even an eight-year-old can already believe he or she is not worthy of love. Later in life it can determine who we become friends with and who we marry. *Self-worth doesn't come from how well we do things. It comes from how well we are spoken to.* Unless we install that special emotional software called respect (different from feeling loved) when they are young, negative self-worth issues will follow them through their development. When we talk-up to our children, we are preparing them to eventually look up to themselves. It fully satisfies our second relationship need, the feeling of being unconditionally valued.

Too often little attention is paid to the parents' tone of voice (our melody) and facial expressions as they impart the information they want their children to have. They are so focused on teaching the lesson that they are unaware of how they come across. *"Get your backpack off the kitchen table!"* Our underlying tone should always be, *"I respect you. I just don't respect what you did!"* Better to say, *"Evan, I know you're relieved to finally be home, but please remove your backpack from our kitchen table so it stays clean. I know you know better. Thank you."* When we talk, our words need to travel past our ears. They need to travel to the heart.

As the esteemed Rabbi Jonathan Sacks (the former Chief Rabbi at the Hebrew Congregation of the Commonwealth in England) reminds us, "Pay close attention to how someone speaks. You can ignore everything else."

Think of certain people you may know, who when they talk to you despite their good intentions, produce this underlying feeling that you're being lectured to with a know-it-all and sarcastic attitude. This is the very opposite of feeling that you have status and are admired. The purpose of their communication is not to inform or even entertain, but to prove how much they know. Not surprisingly, many adults who talk this way have self-worth issues themselves. They are the first to jump at the chance to debate or lecture you in order to win their point of view. They create complexity out of simplicity and live in a constant state of having to prove their worth to others, even their children.

> Pay close attention to how someone speaks. You can ignore everything else

As a clinician, I like to remind parents who come in contact with this type of person not to work so hard to be liked by them. The truth is, they struggle to like themselves.

SELF-WORTH VS. SELF-CONFIDENCE

Parents and educators often confuse self-worth with self-confidence. There is a huge difference in meaning. Self-confidence relates primarily to talent, skills and accomplishments. It's how well we do something. Having self-confidence is, of course, an incredibly important quality and life skill (*Rule Five*). At the same time, we assume that those with self-confidence also have feelings of self-worth. I wish that was always true. There's a difference between feeling good about how well you do something and feeling good about yourself as a person.

What many parents and educators don't recognize, is that doing something well only makes us feel good as it relates to that competence or skill. Making the winning foul shot in the last 5 seconds of a basketball game takes self-confidence, not self-worth. Our self-worth has nothing to do with performance. Nothing. We all know successful people who have achieved tremendous success and status in their professional lives, yet still feel insecure and unworthy inside. *Although they may have achieved high net worth, they can still suffer from low self-worth.*

Self-worth is who we are inside without having to do anything! Too often self-confidence masquerades for self-worth. This becomes a confusing issue when we tell kids that if they get better grades, try out for a team sport or make an extra friend, that they will automatically feel better about themselves. They will, but it doesn't last.

In the context of relationships, what we're really looking for on a deeper level is simply to be accepted for who we are, without having to perform or prove anything, especially with a late bloomer. The self-worth issues of life do not come from the parent-child relationships where children were not loved, but from parent-child relationships where childre were not made to feel admired and valued.

> **There's a difference between feeling good about how well you do something and feeling good about yourself as a person**

Children who lack self-worth can also become more prone to developing future prejudices. They often try to bolster their own worth by finding a person or a group of people who they can put down. An insecure teenager might think, "I may

Rule Two

not be very popular, but I'm smarter or better than those other kids."

Every day our children's self-worth is on the line, including where they attend school. They will compete, sometimes will be made fun of, and will work hard each day to fit in. The truth is, it has always been that way. It is life. However, when children experience a predictable, secure base of acceptance and admiration at home, they will be better inoculated on the multiple fronts they face outside of home. First, they will be more prepared to endure the rejection they will receive from some kids at school or, sadly, even from some teachers. They will also be better prepared to resist the kids who spread risky social behaviors because children with strong self-worth are more capable of turning away from bad influences.

> The self-worth issues of life do not come from the parent-child relationships where children were not loved, but from parent-child relationships where children were not made to feel admired and valued

Social psychologist Jonathan D. Brown suggests, "Self-worth plays its most important role when people confront negative self-relevant experiences, such as personal rejection, criticism from others, or achievement-related failures. These sorts of events lead low self-esteem people to feel humiliated and ashamed of themselves, and to believe they are globally inadequate and bad. People who have always been shown they are valued, on the other hand, do not respond in this way. Rejection, criticism, and failure do not lead them to doubt their worth as a person. *This is the principal value of having self-worth. It allows you to fail without feeling bad about yourself.*" In the context of relationships, when we have low self-worth we tend to settle for less. When we have high self-worth, we settle for more.

REJECT THE BEHAVIOR, NEVER THE CHILD

It helps to remember that children need our deepest respect the most when they deserve it the least. During times of conflict we have a tendency to say things that sound like we are rejecting the whole child, rather than just his behavior. *"You're always selfish." "You never do what I ask."* Global expressions of rejection will make any child or teenager feel, *"All of me is bad!"* We never want to make a child or teenager feel defeated or humiliated. We want to communicate, *"I respect you, I just don't respect what you did!"* We can easily disagree as long as what we say comes with a caring tone and not egotism (which feels humiliating), or sympathy (which can feel victimizing). Our goal should be to help him recover self-control and self-respect. It should not be about showing him who's boss.

> Children need our deepest respect the most when they deserve it the least

"Sammy, I have too much respect for you to allow you to talk to your sister in such a base way. It's not the best of you."

After hearing your eleven-year-old tell you something completely ridiculous, it better to say,

"That's one way to look at it Sam. Let's look together at another way."

This mindful response is very different from saying, "I'm sick and tired of the way you are," and offering up a mini-lecture. Those little "I-told-you-so" mini-lectures are a waste of time because they provide kids with information they already have.

"If you hadn't pushed your brother, you wouldn't be in your room."

"If you had studied, you wouldn't have failed."

Imagine your spouse or friend saying, *"If you hadn't run the red light, you wouldn't have to go to traffic school!"*

An adult doesn't need that kind of information any more than your child does. This kind of shaming and rubbing their

Rule Two

nose in what is an obvious regret, shows complete disrespect. Better to have said,

"Looking back, I have no doubt you would have done it differently."

A basic rule of speaking with respect is to address the situation and not the child's personality.

"Let's hurry," is better than *"Hurry up!"* Or, *"Justin, you know nothing was put away like I asked,"* is far more respectful than, *"This is what you call done?"*

One mother, who, when speaking with her teenage daughter, was more focused on making her point and unwittingly made her daughter feel that her opinions and tastes weren't really worthy of consideration.

"Katie, I wanted to talk with you about how you decorated your room. There's way too many Gothic and depressing posters. The colors are really bad and your room is a downer."

While no doubt Mom was speaking the truth, her tone of voice, facial expression and words conveyed something entire different: "I have no respect for you. You have so many problems."

Mom could have encouraged her daughter to be more open to her feedback by saying:

"Katie, would you mind if we talked for a few minutes about your room. I want to understand more about some of your decisions and your newfound tastes. I know you have reasons for everything you do."

In general, when your child finishes telling you what they want you to know, before saying "YES, BUT" as though you couldn't wait for them to stop talking, I suggest substituting the word, 'AND' to communicate your respect.

"... and is there a way to turn this around?

"... and what if this happens again?"

"... and is there something that will help remind you in the future?"

"... and what would you like me to do?"

Getting children to hear you in the right way is essential for them to respond in the right way. If you want to bring about change faster, *connect before you correct.*

"Derek, you were so focused on putting your new wheels on your skateboard, you weren't able to hear me when I called you to come into the house. That can happen. I know you're capable of doing both."

"Ellen, when you get into a bad mood, you go too far in how you talk and behave. You roll your eyes and become sarcastic. It's not the best of you." Then pause for ten-seconds and lay down the consequence. *"I know you are not surprised that we won't be going out now."* That ten-second calm delay, before laying down the consequence makes a huge difference.

Finally, show some flexibility. When twelve year-old David who just came in from the back yard covered in dirt is told, *"It's obvious you're not in the mood to take a bath now. It takes too much time and you're not even sure you need a bath. You want me to leave it up to you when you want to clean up and smell good. What are some other reasons you don't want to take a bath?"* Wait for his response and sincerely reflect back his reasons.

"David, since you're telling me more of your reasons, let's not do it right now. I'll prepare the bath for later, just the way you like it."

HOW TO TALK WITH RESPECT

KEEP YOUR MELODY HUMBLE

a. **No arrogance, sarcasm, or know-it-all attitudes.** *"Let's hurry,"* is better than, *"Hurry up!"*

b. **You lose trust with a harsh tone.** Keep your cadence (rhythm) slower, your pitch softer (breathier). Think relaxed to sound relaxed.

c. **Admit your own mistakes.** Apologize, using lots of detail about what you did wrong, rather than just saying, *"I'm *sorry."* The detail allows your child to see you really regret what you said or did.

TALK WITH ADMIRATION

a. **Always talk up to your child's potential.** Take them seriously.
"I wonder what you might do about this?"
"Can you think of a way to turn this around?"
"Mmm. Is there another way to solve the problem?"
"That's an interesting way to see it."
"What a dilemma you are in."

b. **Use an expanded vocabulary.**

c. **Connect before you correct.** *"Lenny, would you mind if I made a suggestion?"*
"It's a great quality to finish what you start, but sometimes you need to stop when I call you."

d. **Don't exaggerate.** It destroys trust. *"You're the smartest kid in your class." "Get over it. You act like this is the worst news ever."*

e. **Explain "why."** Do not say, "because I said so." Keep it tight.

f. **Don't lecture.** Talk less, say more.

g. **Use the expressions "I know you understand," or "I know you know that."**
You're telling him he has the intelligence to understand. You show confidence in him to overcome the moment.

h. **Stay flexible and humble.** *"Let me give that some thought."* (wet cement p.42)

i. **Ask for opinions frequently.** *"I would like to know what you think."*

j. **Recognize contributions.** *"Your idea about using the garage really helped."*

SHOW UNCONDITIONAL ACCEPTANCE

a. Allow mistakes without condemnation. Reject the behavior, never the child.
b. If your child struggles, never embarrass or imitate him.
c. Eliminate entirely any comparisons to others.
d. When your child walks into a room, look up and smile warmly.
e. In moments of calm, remind your child of earlier times when things went well.
f. Avoid global expressions of rejection: *"You always forget!" "You never remember!"*

SHOW HEARTFELT APPRECIATION

"Jessica, I really appreciated the way you helped Mom today in the kitchen."

TALKING WITH RESPECT IS A DIALOGUE NOT A MONOLOGUE

Show your 'openness' in the same way you might play ping-pong, with the sole purpose of volleying back-and-forth in order to extend the play. Having a satisfying conversation works in the same way. Don't try to win the point. One way to extend the conversation longer is by asking for your child's opinion. Not as a technique, but with a genuine desire to hear their reasons, even if it's ridiculous. After all, if you respect someone, don't you really

> A conversation is a dialogue, not a monologue or an interview

want to know what they think? A conversation is a dialogue, not a monologue or an interview.

When your child does begin to say more and open up, do not immediately torpedo their feelings or opinions, no matter how far off-base they seem. Think of the process as pouring 'wet cement.' Let him or her feel how open and flexible you are, rather than sounding like you've reached a conclusion that's already set in stone. Besides, you may actually discover a more nuanced position when you learn more. Before you can have a change of heart, you must have a change of perspective. There's a saying: Minds are like parachutes; they work better when they're open.

> Minds are like parachutes; they work better when they're open

I remember reading a powerful sentiment in Dr. Haim Ginott's 1969 book, *Between Parent and Teenager,* revealing a father's lecturing style.

"My father is totally unaware of my real emotions and moods. He does not read between the lines, and cannot sense words unsaid. He can talk at length without ever becoming aware that he has lost his audience. He never notices that he has lost an argument. He merely thinks he has failed to make his position clear. He talks but does not communicate. He teaches and moralizes, and runs most conversations into the ground."

I tell parents, showing a consistent and overwhelming level of respect motivates children's willingness to cooperate and increases their desire to learn. It also sets the natural conditions for children to accept more quickly responsibilities commensurate with their age. Children know the difference when we really want to consider what they have to say, and when we just want to cram down their throats what it is we want them to do.

"Ben, what are some of the reasons I should change my mind about letting you go to your friend for a sleepover?" After listening to his reasons you can say, *"Ben, how about this, for now let's think of it as 'wet cement' and return to our conversation again tonight. We can talk about this as many times as you like. I love talking things through with you."*

"Robert, you think I am totally unfair because I won't let you cut your hair the way you want. You think I don't trust you and I'm making too big a deal about the whole thing. Robert, what am I missing?"

While it's true in the end you probably won't go along with his reasons, you will not diminish his self-respect because you didn't shut-down the conversation prematurely. Put simply, children like any adult, are generally better persuaded after they know you value what they're saying, no matter to what level you disagree. If you immediately start to tell someone all the ways in which they're wrong, there's no incentive to co-operate. But if you start by saying, *"You know what? It's true, what you say about so and so. I agree."* Or, you might say: *"Amanda, would you mind if I suggest another way to look at this?"* Asking permission gives the other a moment to switch mindsets and take in what you are saying. Obviously this approach takes a calm patience.

It's probably becoming very clear at this point that *Rule Two* is the single-most important quality that encourages cooperation and boosts self-worth. Kids can really feel it. Pioneering civil rights activist W.E.B. Du Bois reminds us, *"Children learn more from the way we are, than what we teach."*

The most moving example of how vital it is to feel respected in our homes comes to life in Tim Madigan's Pulitzer Prize-winning book, *I'm Proud of You: Life Lessons From My Friend Fred Rogers*. Nothing else I write on this subject will be as motivating as this vulnerable and gut-warming exchange of letters between these two successful men, and the pain one man carried into his adult life. Tim's level of honesty identifies this striking truth in all of us.

June 22, 1996

Dear Fred,

The purpose of this letter, however, is not to bring you up-to-date on the details of my life, though I am very glad to do so. The purpose, Fred, is that I have something to ask of you. The last several years have been a very profound time of intense personal pain and

Rule Two

great healing, a time of great self-discovery as I've tried to come to terms with the realities of my life past and present.

At the forefront of my mind and soul right now, is how hard I tried to get my dad to be proud of me, through sports, through school, through the way I tried to be obedient and good. But no matter what I did, it never seemed enough.

I could never wrest from him the love and sense of acceptance that I so desperately craved as a child, and have been craving ever since. I realize now that God is the ultimate source for that kind of love and acceptance. But I also have realized that I have gravitated toward older men in my life, without really knowing why.

There are several men older than me who have become very important in my life. And one by one I plan on asking them this. "Will you be proud of me?" That is the question I have for you this morning, Fred. Will you be proud of me?

It would mean a great deal to me if you would. I have come to love you in a very special way. In your letters, and during our brief time together in Pittsburgh, you have done so much to teach me how to be a good person and man. And now I have this favor to ask of you. Will you be proud of me?
With much love and gratitude,

Tim

July 1, 1996

Dear Tim,

The answer to your question is: YES, a resounding YES, I will be proud of you. I am proud of you. I have been proud of you since first we met. I'm deeply touched that you would offer so much of yourself to me and I look forward to knowing all that you care to share in the future. Nothing you could tell me could ever change my YES for you. Please remember that.

I wonder if you realize how special you really are? Your place in this life is unique, absolutely unique. I feel blessed to be one of your friends. Only God can arrange such mutually trusting relationships. For sure! For sure!! YES, Tim. YES. I will be proud of you.

Love,
Fred

Want to hear more examples of how to talk with respect? I encourage you see the extraordinary documentary movie, "Won't You Be My Neighbor," produced by Yo Yo Ma's son, Nicholas Ma. I also encourage you to order the entire episode series for your younger children (ages 4 to 10) to watch and grow with. Mr. Rogers was truly the grand master of relationships for all generations. He was famous for saying. *"The outside of a child's life has changed a lot, but the inside of a child's life hasn't changed at all."*

TAKING BACK OUR WORDS

Although our words account for only about 10% of our real message, we should still choose them very, very carefully, the way a master chef chooses his/her ingredients to achieve great taste.

> Sarcasm is a caustic contaminant that chips away at trust and self-worth

It's difficult to take words back. As adults, we can say things we didn't mean and then offer a heartfelt apology and move on. Not so with children and teenagers.

Rule Two

Name calling and sarcasm sticks, even once! Children come to believe that deep down we meant what we regretted saying. Sarcasm is a caustic contaminant that chips away at trust and self-worth. It is a game of one-upmanship, producing one winner and one loser. It works for the great comedians on stage who make us laugh, but not for great relationships. A sarcastic tone will train a child or teenager to be hard, critical and suspicious. It also creates feelings of shame. The antidote for shame is respect.

Like medicine in a bottle, I wish certain words came with a warning label. Caution: Certain words have side-effects. We all know by now that anger is a weak man's substitute for strength. It is also a secondary emotion. Below anger are the real underlying issues that are bothering us, such as fear, shame and guilt.

When a father of four children is watching his 13-year-old daughter struggle with being scattered and disorganized, he seizes the moment to control his upset and show his respect.

"Lindsey, don't worry about not knowing where your science book is. We're a team and we'll find it together. Forgetting where your book is —is not a big deal." Lindsey's father knows that being organized is a skill like math or science. Some kids have a natural talent for it and some don't. It shouldn't be a reason to be angry. It's not the end of the world to be disorganized. Besides, we usually find the right people in life to help us, be it in marriage, friendship or business. Optimism avoids feelings of "learned helplessness."

The antidote for shame is respect

Although remaining calm will always serve your child or teen best, there are times when showing real anger and outrage is both natural and called for. The key is to limit the thunder of your upset to less than 30 seconds, and no more than once a month, maximum. Obviously the circumstances must warrant your outrage. With a very angry tone, you can say: *"Stacy, I am furious at the nasty names you called your sister. Leave this room right now! When you are back in control of yourself, we will start again. I know you will make it right with your sister."*

There is a big difference between *losing your temper* and

using your temper. Showing anger is a part of all human expression, and the ability to show how you regain your self-control quickly is a wonderful lesson. It also reinforces the secure feeling that your child is always safe with you. Like most things in life, there are always exceptions. If your child shows a defiant pattern of anger, resist expressing any signs of anger and instead follow the guiding principles under The Difficult Child *(page 129).*

"Alex, let's try an experiment. Just walk into the restaurant. Then, if you don't like it, we can walk out."

YES, TODDLERS CAN FEEL RESPECT TOO

Although most of this chapter concerns middle-grade children and teenagers, I want to touch upon the principle of respect in the context of toddlers. We pass them around like little footballs without batting an eye. We smile dismissively when they're upset. We stick a binky in their mouth when we want to silence them. We call them silly nicknames. We talk about them in front of others as though they're not present. *"Sam is being shy now." "Allison was cranky all day." "Bobby is my little monkey."* Research shows that feelings of embarrassment begin as early as 18 months. *"David, do you have a poopy diaper, I smell it from here."*

Pioneering educator Leontine Young makes this profound insight: "The smaller the person, the less we worry about his dignity. Sometimes, we even find the idea a little ludicrous, as if smallness and inexperience were incompatible with anything so majestic as human dignity...*Yet children have a great sense of their own dignity. They couldn't define what it is, but they know when it has been violated."*

When three-year-old Caroline runs away from Grandma after being told to kiss her good-bye, Caroline should be told by her mother, "You don't want to kiss Grandma now, maybe later."

When four-year-old Angela points to a light bulb and asks, "Daddy, what's this?" "It's a light bulb Angelica."

Resist infantilizing her by turning everything into a feeling session. *"Angela, I can see you are curious about what this is."* Rather, just answer the question. *"It's a light bulb, Angela. It goes under the lamp shade. When it's turned on, it makes the room bright. Here's the switch that controls it. Let's practice it together."*

Showing respect, especially with younger children also means never trying to fool or take advantage of them. I have seen mothers trick their children with promises never kept, bribe them with goodies, or worse, just fake them out totally by saying things that are totally untrue.

"Danny get in the car now and you will find your bottle there!" One mother, in an effort to get her four-year-old son in the car, told him, *"David, let's go to Aunt Ellen's now."* Instead, they went to the supermarket. Trust is something that should never be negotiated away.

When a situation arises when you can't do something, just reflect your child's need in a quiet caring way (and mean it). *"Kenny, I know you are really hungry and you're tired of waiting for me to make you that sandwich. In three minutes I'm going to make it exactly the way you like it."*

Six-year-old Claire was crying for more attention, her mother who had read *Reset*, knew just how and what to say:

"Claire, I need to change your brother's diaper first, then I will be able to give you my full attention. I want to hear everything you want me to know. I'm coming right back to you. Thank you, Claire."

Being spoken to consistently with respect, creates an active feeling of self-worth that is always present. Without respect we devalue and dehumanize the other. Some parents who catch themselves in the moment sounding disrespectful will try to over-correct and immediately switch gears, using praise to reset the direction of the conflict. Unfortunately, praise won't work for two reasons. First, it will appear unnatural and forced. Second, praise requires performance. You must do something first to earn it.

There are many well meaning advice-givers who believe we pay too much attention to our children's feelings. They believe you don't need to give reasons to a two-year-old, just consequences.

They're just plain wrong! The child may stop for the moment

out of fear, but you will lose a deeper connection over time. Front-load heaps of respect, without caving in (Rule Four) and you will continue to boost your child's self-worth.

"Katie, I respect how you feel and can not go along with what you want, I know deep down you respect what I am saying. I know what a turn-off I am to you now and I can feel your anger. I hope in time you will see things differently."

We also never want to sound singsongy. Telling a four-year-old in a sing-songy drawn-out tone of voice, "Henry, it's time to have lunch. Come in now and then you can go back outside to play, okay?"

Just spacing out those words and imagining those sing-songy sounds is making me feel nauseous. No doubt you can think of more than one person right now who uses that same tone and rhythm with adults too. It shows much more respect when we give the information in a simple, straight forward, caring tone. Remember, your goal is promote respect and self-mastery, not feelings of dependence. Although the intention is loving, the tone can be heard as a talking down.

Even reading a fun children's book out-loud should be read in the natural ways we would express the normal emotional language of words or pictures we see on a page. Talking in a sing-songy way also sends mixed signals when later you want them to snap into action and cooperate. *"C'mon Henry, we're headed to Grandma's. I'll meet you downstairs."* For some, sounding sing-songy can make a parent feel, "See how nice I am."

TANTRUMS

When we're out in public, we can feed into a child's tantrum by thinking an audience of strangers will be so embarrassing to them that they will stop. They won't. When this happens, it is best to physically pick-up your child and carry him out saying (in a caring tone), *"I know how upset you are. I wanted us to talk in private so you won't feel embarrassed in front of all those people. I won't be able to buy you the toy you want. I came to the*

Rule Two

store only to get shampoo. I know how upset you are and that you're furious with me."

Your toddler may not know the exact meaning of what you're saying, but he will at a deeper level feel you take his upset seriously. Stay with this strategy before you go back in. Maintain a high level of empathy. Be patient as you wait out his tantrum with respect. Yes, it will take a few more minutes and many rounds, but you are laying the foundation for respect and connection. Louis Pasteur said it best: *"When I approach a child, I carry two sentiments – a tenderness for who he is and a respect for what he may become."*

EXPRESSIONS THAT SHOW RESPECT

"If there is something you need, come and tell me."

Said with a caring tone of voice. This is a great expression that encourages openness without fear of consequences.

"I do not want to play that game."

Use this repeated expression when a child starts to get cranky and whine out of boredom or manipulation Use the expression, *"Nicki, I don't want to play that game. I know you can control yourself."* Say it calmly and respectfully. No sarcasm. Repeat when necessary. *"Nicki, I don't want to play that game. I know you can control yourself."*

"Let me make a note of that."

A very powerful communication expression that shows complete respect. Something remembered or written down impresses the child that you are taking his matter seriously.

"Let me give that some thought."

This can be used when a parent does not want to be rushed into an answer on the spot. "_____,I want to think it through before I give you my decision. I know you want a decision right now, but it would be unfair to your brother and sister. I would never do that to you either."

"_____, I'm going to think about this. Let's both think about it. When we see each other tonight, we can talk about it again. Does that sound like a good plan?"

"I was wondering if you would be willing to try an experiment?"

This is a great way to make your child feel open to new ideas. It also allows the child to fail without feeling defeated, since it was only an experiment. "Sherry, would you be willing to try an experiment?

Rule Three

PROMOTE A FAMILY CULTURE OF TRUTH
▼
SELF-AWARENESS

*You cannot force someone to comprehend
a message that they are not ready to receive.
Still, you must never underestimate the power of planting a seed.*
—ANONYMOUS

Frequently, young children do not always know or recognize how they feel until we give them the right language to identify those feelings. Parents assume kids always know what they're feeling. For example, when they're jealous, angry, sad, even happy. Yes, they have those feelings but they often don't recognize them in that moment. When we model honest feedback, given with care and respect, we build self-awareness. This process of giving honest descriptive feedback begins very early in family development. It is how we first learn about ourselves in relation to others. Learned self-awareness also helps us develop empathy. The more we help a child discover how they feel (emotionally and physically), the more they will begin to recognize those same emotions in others.

However, we must keep in mind that a family culture of truth will *not* be accepted unless children consistently experience feeling deeply respected (*Rule Two*). Truth without trust can destroy relationships. Obviously, receiving feedback must be free from sarcasm, manipulation, arrogance or trickery. Even a two-year-old can begin to gain a sense of self-awareness when you describe their behavior with respect.

> What makes trust so vital is that it also leads to faith; faith in ourselves and faith in our parents

"David, you get upset when I take you out of your car seat too quickly. You want me to go slower."

If children are not taught when they are very young how to become self-aware, it becomes very unnatural later in life to hear about their behaviors and makes them feel more defensive and hostile to others. As a result, truth is taken as criticism. Learned self-awareness allows children to build on their strengths, as well as face their own inborn existential struggles, whether they have learning differences, are perfectionistic, impulsive, lazy, gifted or just average.

Giving direct, heartfelt emotional and physical feedback to your child or teenager demonstrates a belief in his or her ability to change. It signals that you are willing to sacrifice being liked for the moment, for the value of being honest. Being diplomatic in the real world is smart. Being diplomatic with your child is not smart. It reflects a good heart, but not a good way. Before we can change something, we must become aware of it.

"Lucy, when you get into a bad mood, you go too far in how you talk and behave. You roll your eyes and become sarcastic. It's not the best of you."

It is why author and inspirational speaker Ken Blanchard says: *"Feedback is the breakfast of champions."* A family culture of truth should be modeled and promoted every day as a core value, as you would hard work or a religious belief.

There is, however, a membership fee. You have to be able to take the truth in order to tell the truth! Some parents are good at dishing it out, but can't take it in. Before we can teach self-awareness, we have to first be self-aware and self-correcting ourselves as parents. You can tell a lot about a person by the way they handle feedback, both positive and negative. One father who understood how to model a culture of truth, told his teenage daughter:

Rule Three

> **Being able to receive valuable feedback with an open-mind is a central characteristic of maturity**

"Wow! I had no idea I sounded that way. Now I see why you don't open up to me."

Another daughter quietly said,

"Daddy, you scare me. Your face always looks angry."
"Jessica, I didn't realize I look so scary. I know you were afraid to tell me. It's terrible the way I make you feel." Then, with a warm smile, *"I will stop making those angry faces."*

Being able to receive valuable feedback with an open-mind is a central characteristic of maturity. I tell those who attend my "Parenting Without Therapy™" workshops, "I'm not trying to send you to a psychiatrist, I'm trying to send you to a mirror."

NO WALKING ON EGGSHELLS

When we promote a family culture of truth, there is no eggshell-walking. Ever! No one walks around with that queasy feeling, thinking, "I'd better not say anything, I don't want to start a fight," "be laughed at" or, "be misunderstood." Family members are free to say how they feel and what they think to one another.

Sixteen year-old Stacy is told by her mother, *"You're still angry at me from last night. You're not ready to forgive me."*

Four-year-old Adam hears his dad say, *"Adam, you don't want to let go of your toy now. You want to control everything, even me."*

When 8-year-old Robert rolls his eyes at his younger brother, his father tells him, *"Robert, the truth is sometimes you are jealous of David and you like to get him in trouble."* Robert answers, *"No, I don't, he makes all the trouble."* Then his father says, *"You know in our family we always tell each other the truth. I know deep down you know the truth."*

> The problem with conformity is that everyone will like you, except yourself

Part of the reason to start this process early, is that as we get older we can't always count on others to give us the right feedback, or at the right time. It can get a little more tricky because unfortunately not all the feedback we hear may be true. We may be influenced to change, just to feel accepted. The balance between conformity and preserving our essential individuality is a critical life lesson. As author Rita Mae Brown reminds us, "The problem with conformity is that everyone will like you, except yourself!" Being brought up with a *family culture of truth* will make it much easier to know how to tell the difference between truth and fiction because we will have heard it before.

When we have emotional trust, which is the premise of this entire book, receiving honest feedback becomes a very positive experience. *The more feedback we are able to give and receive to one another, the closer the relationship. The less feedback we give and receive, the more distant the relationship.* In all my family therapy sessions, I have one motto: "The truth, the whole truth and nothing but the truth."

It takes a patient parent to unravel upset. Not everyone has the appetite to do this. For some, moving on and getting past the conflict is the goal. Little concern is given to the long-term negative effect that comes from avoiding searching for the truth.

I'm certainly *not* suggesting that you start giving personal feedback to others outside your core family. Not at all. Going around and telling others about their personal behaviors will be taken as arrogant attempts to control their behavior and how they should feel. You would be told in a condescending way, 'Mind your own business." The world runs on results and performance, not feelings, and that's how it should be. By core family I am referring *only* to your children and spouse, unless, of course, your extended family and closest friends also share the same *culture of truth* values.

Rule Three

BE THE SPORTS ANNOUNCER

I would like to suggest a transformative metaphor that will make it easier to narrate your child's world whether outside of the house or around the kitchen table. Imagine yourself as a sports announcer giving a play by play description of what's happening in the moment. A sports announcer's description is so vivid and accurate, that the listener has little doubt about what's going on. *"Danny, look at that family sitting at the table next to us. The father's face is filled with anger, and the mother is pretending everything is okay. No one at the table is talking to each other. They are all silent. I feel terrible for those two little boys because they probably feel alone. That would never happen in our family."*

"Michael, look at that little boy over there on the bench sharing his potato chips with that boy. He sure knows how to be a friend. You can see the other boy likes the way he is doing that by the expression and smile on his face. You can even see him licking his lips because he likes the taste too."

"Look, Carolyn, at that little girl over there in the corner. She looks worried." Or, *"See that man standing by the cash register, he sure looks impatient and wants the woman to hurry-up."*

Parents report that this psychological metaphor eases their anxieties during times of conflict and confusion. Reality television doesn't just come from a flat screen. It comes as soon as we walk out our front doors. Unlike TV where we can turn-off a program, we can't turn-off the world. Nor should we. Sometimes parents remain silent too long with the hopes that the problem just goes away. When we're silent too long, we look out of touch and void our leadership role. These are prime opportunities to bring understanding and empathy to your children by describing and narrating what they see or experience. Without your input, your child will either guess at what is happening, or worse, other people with different values may teach an entirely different life lesson. False conclusions create anxiety and faulty thinking. This approach helps children learn faster about how the world works and how people work.

Knowing just what to say or do will powerfully shape your children's values and behaviors. Think of it as observational learning. A word of caution: Don't go on and on. Fifteen-to thirty-second sound bites will usually do the trick.

When a five-year-old in a mall sees a toddler throwing a tantrum. You might narrate it this way:

"Jeffrey, you see that little girl crying over there? She's crying because her mom doesn't realize she wants to get out of the stroller and walk for herself. Her mom is not in tune with her the way I am with you. I know you feel bad for the little girl. Me too."

Many parents ignore those uncomfortable moments, trying to whisk their kids past them. This can happen for example when we pass an inappropriate billboard.

"Sam, I'm sorry you had to see that disturbing billboard. It is disturbing for me too. It's disgusting to see adults who dress half-naked. They have very different values than our family. When we pass it again, let's not look at it!"

Children see, hear and feel things that are ripe for explanation. Resist the politically correct propaganda that says, 'do not make value judgments about other people's behavior.' There's a big difference between gossip just to put other people down, and talking openly with empathy and respect about what children see. While we want our children to experience all that is good in life, it is unavoidable that they will also see and hear much that is not at all good and disturbing. Life for young children can be like watching a foreign film without subtitles. It is virtually impossible for them to understand the full meaning or partial meaning when behaviors are complex. Without your input, your child will either guess at what is happening, or worse, other people with different values may teach an entirely different life lesson at a later time. False conclusions create anxiety and faulty thinking. It is the perfect time to narrate the world the way you would narrate a foreign film. You can also practice this exercise when you are looking at family photographs, books, magazines and videos. Life is a class no child wants to miss.

Rule Three

Done with wisdom and age appropriateness, being a *sports announcer* and narrating their world will become one of the most powerful opportunities to teach children about empathy and explain the world. On a daily basis you want to be training your children to think psychologically.

"David, look at that man on the sidewalk talking to himself and acting crazy. Look at the crazy faces he is making. He is mentally ill and needs help. Something happened to him in his life that we don't know about. He needs professional care. Soon the police will come and try to help him."

Many parents consciously ignore those uncomfortable moments, trying to whisk their kids past them. This can also happen for example when you might be at your favorite retail mall and you see people dressed in sexually inappropriate ways. It's the perfect time to quietly say:

"Lucy, it can feel embarrassing to see people who dress half-naked. They have little self-respect for themselves and do not mind drawing attention to themselves in such a way. They have such different values than our family."

"Jonathan, after hearing about Jason at school, it is obvious he has serious psychological problems. He is a bully and because he is really insecure, he wants to be first to put others down. Let's come up with something to say to him so you will be prepared next time. Even if it doesn't stop him, saying something back will give you self-respect. Staying silent will make you feel weak inside. We can practice this together so you will feel confident. Do you like this idea?"

Wearing the *sports announcer* hat also allows parents to verbally track each child from across a kitchen table, or across a room. Successful teachers use this strategy too in their classrooms. *"Jenna, I'm attending to Bobby now. As soon as I am finished you will have my full attention. I want to hear everything you want me to know. Thank you."*

THE HALLMARK OF A GREAT RELATIONSHIP

Family members who emotionally trust each other will not process feedback as disloyalty or criticism, but rather as a very valuable life gift. The act of giving honest emotional feedback is a deeply considerate act of love. It is as though you are happy you're the messenger and you have the good fortune of saying it! Honest feedback is the hallmark of a great relationship.

"Daryl, I am noticing the way you clench your mouth when you get upset! Your whole face tightens up! I know it makes you uncomfortable. Next time just tell me in words what you are feeling."

"Justin, it's true, I do sometimes favor your sister and that's going to stop!"

"Mom, it's true, I blamed you for my bad mood this morning, but it was me all along."

When we are emotionally safe, we can talk this way. This Yiddish proverb says it all: "A half-truth is still a whole lie." Too often we are so caught up in keeping the peace that we stop telling the truth. Later in life, it will also define what kind of friends your children will seek out. A good friend accepts you as you are, while a great friend helps make you better. When we stop caring we stop giving feedback.

Think about some of your own friends and family and how much you hold back so as not to risk losing that relationship. You can determine the quality of each friendship just from that honest exercise. Some friends pretend they want honest feedback and, when they are offered the unvarnished truth, they become angry, resentful and defensive. As the brilliant 18th century existential philosopher, Arthur Schopenhauer

> A good friend accepts you as you are, while a great friend helps make you better

Rule Three

reminds us, *"All truth passes through three stages. First, it is ridiculed. Second, it is violently opposed. Third, it is accepted as being self-evident."*

The three key qualities that determine an individual's capacity for healthy close relationships are:

1. *Comfortable in examining their behaviors with others.*
2. *Comfortable in being honest with others.*
3. *Comfortable in accepting feedback.*

What do all defensive people have in common? They *never* ask, "What am I missing? "What don't I see?" What is it that I've done to cause such upset?" Their default reaction is, "It's not my fault, it's yours!" It's as though when they drive a car and arrive at their destination they think everything's okay. What they don't realize is how many cars they hit while getting there. It's astonishing how unaware so many people are in the ways they affect others. In their minds they believe they come across natural, relaxed and relatable. They are unaware of their tone of voice, or how awkward, negative or draining they can be. The antidote for a lack of self-awareness is promoting a family culture of truth.

THE MOST POWERFUL WAY TO GIVE CHILDREN FEEDBACK

The single most powerful method for activating self-awareness is called *Reveal the Motivation*. Every action of a child has a purpose. Part of our job is to figure out their motivation or purpose, and reveal it out loud. This rarely-used communication strategy accelerates a child's self-awareness.

"Emily, just because Benny won't try your oatmeal cereal, you don't have to make faces and go into a bad mood. It creates *bad feelings for everyone."*

"Robert, when I describe everyone's behavior at the table, it annoys you. You want me to stop doing that!"

Five-year-old Alan hears his mother say, *"You like pushing your sister so you can control her. In our family we only use our words."*

"Lilly, the truth is your bad mood started this morning in the kitchen when your sister didn't want to make pancakes with you. You kept your angry face so she won't talk to you."

When a parent reveals a child's hidden emotional goal and then reflects it back immediately, a teaching window will open for that child to look at his behavior. Parents should use this strategy with humility and precision. It requires both a high level of insight and an elegant delivery. In that moment of revealing a child's motivation, the parent assumes a certain magician-like quality—a mentalist of sorts. *"Dina, you want to be the boss of your sister. You want to make her go outside with you."*

For example, a child seeking the goal of attention might be confronted with:

"Simon, I can see that you are happiest when I am busy only with you, not your brother."

Or, *"Laura, you want to be left alone tonight rather than change your mood and be with the family."*

Say that, rather than continue to debate; simply say once or twice what you want your child to know, and then end with, "I know you know the truth." Let your child have the last word. Even a four-year-old is more than capable of recognizing a truth about their behavior. If the parent's insight is accurate, the child will typically respond with a smile and almost blush with a twinkle in his eye, becoming aware of himself. I call this honest self-awareness a recognition reflex.

Parents should *'reveal the child's motivation'* with complete humility, with the goal of reaching the heart and not the head. We remember less than 15% of what we hear, and 85% of what we see and feel! Never communicate a sense of superiority or attempt to embarrass or shame, with an "I-found-you-out" attitude. It will render your insight useless, and instead become a flashpoint for

Rule Three

anger causing your child to dig in and act out.

Another way you can lower your child's resistance to hearing the truth is by using the expression *"Part of you."* For example, *"Michelle, part of you doesn't want to be with the family tonight."* or *"Jason, part of you doesn't want to hear the truth about your bad temper this afternoon."* Saying, *"Part of you"* preserves your child's self-respect. Contrast that to *"Your bad temper ruins everything!"*

> We remember less than 15% of what we hear, and 85% of what we see and feel!

A word of caution: *Make sure you are 110% sure before you use Reveal the Motivation.* If you are wrong about your insight, a child will react even more negatively, thus reinforcing a lack of understanding and creating an even larger divide between both of you. You will lose their trust. The child will think, "You really don't know me." Never take the risk if you are not 110% on the money. If in doubt, leave it out! Wait for another time. I promise, it's right around the corner.

However, when you are right, do not retreat from your insight. Briefly repeat what you know to be true. Do not be influenced if you get a dirty look or a blank stare. Stay relaxed and calm. With a serious look, say, *"I know you know it's true."* If your child says, *"No it isn't,"* repeat it once more.

"Jackson, I know you know it's true," and let it go. You want to be seen as comfortable when *s*peaking the truth. Do not enter into a debate. Let your child have the last word. You can't force a child to have a conversation about an experience if they're not ready!

"Alan, we had a rough afternoon together today. You lost your control when things didn't go the way you wanted. Let's talk about it again later."

I can think of one wonderful 11-year-old-girl who excelled in writing. It was obvious she had a passion for storytelling. She was also self-motivated and perfectionistic. Although her parents were more than aware of her zoning out during family dinners, frequently being moody and avoiding having social relationships, they were caught up in her dream. Instead of helping her face her obsessive ways, they showered her with everything she needed to feed her dream and her habits. Her parents walked on eggshells in fear she would get upset. Later, she would develop an eating disorder.

Then there was Jonathan, a very smart 14-year-old boy who found himself drawn to writing software code for computer games. He had very little interest in school and even less interest in any social activity. Like so many talented children, his parent's were unable to re-direct him to be more socially-minded and self-aware. Both his parents thought this was just a stage. Later, he would find himself experiencing a mild nervous break-down.

Early on, both sets of parents might have had a conversation that went something like this:

"Jonathan, Mom and I are so happy you have discovered something about yourself you love doing. You really have a natural talent with computers." After your child takes in the feedback, you might add: *"Mom and I also have noticed that when you are with the family, you drift off as if you are going into your own world. You show less and less caring attention to your brother and sister, and you don't express your emotions the way you used to. You are going more and more into your own world. We know how exciting it is to work on your software program, but you seem more nervous then ever before. Does this ring true? (Pause) Jonathan, nothing is more important to mom and I than your emotional health. Nothing! Not school, getting job, winning the awards you have. Nothing! All these wonderful accomplishments mean nothing to Mom and I, without your emotional health. You know in your heart what we are saying is true. Unless you are able to make these personal changes we are talking about now, Mom and I are going to insist you take a break from your computer interest. That's how much we respect and love you. Sure we want you to be successful, but only if you get back into a healthy emotional life."*

Be prepared to prove to your child that their emotional development is far more important than any accomplishment, goal or skill they may have. This is not a one-time conversation. Each day we need to emphasize our children's psychological development.

HOW TO PROMOTE A FAMILY CULTURE OF TRUTH

MODEL SELF-AWARENESS AND SELF-CORRECTION

Admit your mistakes quickly and sincerely.

Wouldn't it be great if self-awareness worked the way spell-check works? You would have perpetual mindfulness that automatically adjusts when your tone of voice, facial expressions, body language or vocabulary gets off-track. To help stay mindful, each time you want to communicate something important, ask yourself this question: In this moment, how do I want to come across? Without self-awareness we experience emotions as happening to us, not realizing it can really be chosen by us.

Even as I am writing this paragraph, I'm automatically asking myself a series of questions to stay respectful. Is my style humble or arrogant? Am I lecturing or am I informing? Does my tone and vocabulary convey warmth and respect, or just technical jargon? Do I sound like a know-it-all? Within split seconds of coming to those answers, I make adjustments. As we listen to ourselves talk, we should try to make those adjustments in real time. It may sound fatiguing to think this way, but sooner than you think the process will become super easy and more natural. Learned self-awareness is a gradual process.

Remember when you first got your driver's license and you were hyper-focused on remaining alert to every detail of your driving experience: how much acceleration, braking, rotating your head before you change lanes, backing up, and 50 other things. You didn't even want the radio on for fear of distraction. Your only goal was remaining alert. After ten minutes of driving, you were exhausted! Yet, in only a matter of months you were more relaxed. Within a year, staying alert was effortless. Similarly, becoming self-aware becomes more natural and automatic over time.

It also helps if we feel a certain sense of disgust when we discover unattractive traits about ourselves, especially if that behavior is hurtful to someone we respect and love. That disgust should not be misused to put ourselves down, but to motivate us to change faster. When we are so turned off by our own actions, we become less defensive and are ready to change faster.

Hearing a child tell us, *"Mom, sometimes your faces and mood makes me not want to be with you!"* is a real wake-up call.

In my own clinical practice, I often videotape parts of our sessions (with permission, of course) in order to allow parents to see how they sometimes look and sound. To better evaluate your own openness and level of self-reflection, here are two simple questions.

How much do I love hearing feedback about myself from my family and friends?

1. *Often*
2. *Rarely*
3. *Never*
4. *Always*

How often do I ask my family and friends for feedback about myself?

1. *Often*
2. *Rarely*
3. *Never*
4. *Always*

Rule Three

To help look at yourself in a more honest way, do not think in terms of judging yourself, think in terms of *evaluating* yourself. This exercise is more than semantics. The word *judging* feels like finger-pointing and tends to evoke early negative memories of being criticized or made to feel not good enough. Judging feels like an all-or-nothing experience, making us feel either all good or all bad, all right or all wrong. It also can lead to quitting a task faster.

In contrast, when you think in terms of evaluating yourself, it's not an all-or-nothing experience. Evaluating allows you to measure your skills or behavior on a continuum, like a rating scale. It provides for varying degrees to calibrate what you need to know. It also helps you focus on the smaller details in order to change or improve. The word evaluate has a much more relaxed sound and context. As your children get older, teach them the difference between judging and evaluating themselves as they live a life of self-reflection.

KEEP YOUR MELODY HUMBLE

As long as what is said comes with a caring tone and not egotism (which feels abusive or humiliating) or sympathy (which can feel victimizing), your feedback will not be taken as criticism. Your tone of voice must be compassionate and elegant, as if one is trying hard to reach *only* the heart and not the head. You want to talk with admiration. *When attitudes are hostile, facts are unconvincing.* Never convey a sense of superiority, with "I gotcha" or an "I-found-you-out" tone and attitude.

"Ally, we all can see the sour face you are making. The truth is you are in a bad mood and don't want to go. I know you don't like to be this way either." If your feedback is rejected, you will know you have more *trust* work ahead of you.

Some parents try too hard to prove they're right. They battle and debate every point. This egotistical approach leaves a trail of bitterness. Giving feedback is not hammering away non-stop in order to win.

You simply say once or twice what you want your child to know, and then say, "I know you know the truth." Be clear, concise and caring. Remember, *Our melody* decisively determines how other people feel about us and the level of trust we project. *You can feel a look more powerfully than words.*

GIVE FEEDBACK FREQUENTLY AND SPONTANEOUSLY

Speak the truth frequently and spontaneously. Don't hold back. Learned self-awareness comes from frequent feedback given with respect. When we get uncomfortable, sometimes we sandwich the negative feedback between two compliments. Hedging communicates that the other person is weak and that you have no respect for them. With each passing day, seek every opportunity to provide positive recognition, not praise, on their progress. *"You are well on your way to breaking your bad mood habit."*

"Stacy, your giggling made your brother feel that you don't care. I know you do care. I noticed sometimes when you don't know what to say, you giggle. True or not true?"

"Matthew, when you don't get your way, you get into a bad mood. Despite your strong feelings, I know you can control them."

"Jonathan, I love the way you closed the car door so quietly."

NEVER EXAGGERATE

Nothing erodes trust and credibility faster than exaggeration. Use the right adjectives to accurately describe all behaviors, including your own. *"You always think of yourself first." "This is the worst thing you've ever done." "You're going to give me a heart attack."* Avoid talking in absolutes (*never* or *always*). Make it only about the behavior, not their personality.

Rule Three

EXPRESS APPRECIATION IN BOTH DIRECTIONS

This applies in both directions, when you give feedback and when you receive it. *"Alex, I really respect your openness in how you took in what I said about your bad mood this morning with your sister."* Or, *"Thank you so much for letting me know I was sarcastic. It really helps me to stay self-aware so I don't turn you off."*

HOW TO INTRODUCE A CULTURE OF TRUTH FOR THE FIRST TIME

Begin today by announcing to your children a new way of talking – a fresh start, so to speak. Do not just begin speaking with a culture of truth. It requires a set-up and introduction.

"Kids, Mom and I are going to start talking in a new way. We used to ignore bad behavior and the truth about what we all see. From now we are only going to say things that are true and if anyone in the family doesn't like it, we are still going to continue. We want you to have complete freedom to tell us everything, anytime and anywhere. We want to start what we call, a family culture of truth. If we roll our eyes at each other, or someone is sarcastic or someone says something that is not true, we will point it out.

This includes us as your parents. We are sorry we did not do this with you for so many years. It was a big mistake. We didn't know how to talk honestly. Now we do. The reason for our change is due to a book we recently bought. We've heard a lot about this book and the author, and we trust his ideas 100%. You'll probably see the book around the house. It's going to make us all feel closer to each other."

When you begin it is very common for children to resist the process and remain defensive and stubborn. Let your children know: *"In the beginning it will feel weird to talk this way, but soon it will become natural for all of us."* No more walking on eggshells." The reason to mention the book is because kids become curious as to why things are changing. Now they will know. By talking about it, we show ourselves to be wide open for discussion. Even when we say things that are positive, some children may not always believe us. They doubt us because too many times we have said things we don't mean in order to get them to do things we want.

Then, enthusiastically say:

"Kids, let start with me, can you tell me what really bothers you about the way I am? Be brutally honest. Am I typically relaxed or do I sound angry a lot? Are you ever afraid of me? Tell me if you think I'm a moody mother. I am going to take it all in. I promise, no resistance! Do not worry about hurting my (our) feelings. We want the real truth. No more walking on eggshells! Talking freely about your feelings will help us trust each other more. It will make us all closer."

Hearing parents authentically and enthusiastically seek out feedback about their own behaviors is the fastest way to accelerate a new *family culture of truth*. If you have *not* been living with a family culture of truth, your children may initially be uncomfortable in bringing up a past pattern or a serious issue. If this is your case, I suggest that you bring one up, and then with a heartfelt regret, you can say:

"Amanda, do you mind if I tell you something that has been heavy on my heart for months? I remember the time I picked you up from school, and you wanted to stop and get pizza. I'm sure you remember that. I was in such a bad mood, and took it out on you. I remember giving you a phony excuse about why I couldn't go. The truth is, I was selfish. I know I have done this to you before. I get very moody sometimes for no reason. From the bottom of my heart I am so sorry. Please forgive me."

This kind of acknowledgement and self-awareness will rebuild trust. Keep in mind because this is your first talk, it might start a little rough. Because you have arbitrarily chosen this time to talk, your kids may not be in the mood to talk about it. You may only hear the sound of crickets at first. Stay with it, but don't force it. The initial introduction *for a culture of truth* typically lasts between five to fifteen minutes. The more important point is that you've announced a whole new way of speaking the truth to each other.

Finally, once you set the example of talking this way, hold yourself accountable in maintaining your own self-awareness. You cannot continue to ask your children to look at themselves honestly if you are not held to the same standard. Inconsistency will make your relationship, as well as their behaviors, go into decline. Once you've established a *culture of truth*, you can talk in shorthand. Before leaving the house you can remind your son or daughter, *"Let's do a mood check!"*

YES, BRING UP THE PAST (REPEATED FROM RULE ONE)

In addition to knowing how to acknowledge what is happening in the moment, we must also know how to acknowledge and express was has happened in the past, especially if a relationship is in need of repair or a reset. The elephant in the room is something we have all experienced.

Whether it was a silly fight that was never really resolved, a trauma, or a consistent pattern of emotional neglect, the challenge becomes knowing how to bring up past hurts. Often when this happens, we walk on eggshells in order to avoid making things worse.

Most parents are so relieved it is already in the past and even more relieved to leave it there. The problem with this pattern is that it makes the person who is hurting want to give up on the relationship. To help us get through those roadblocks and give voice to 'the elephant in the room,' we must put aside our discomfort, ego and vulnerability in order to communicate past hurts. As literary award winner and author, John Green so poignantly reminds us, *"That's the thing about pain, it demands to be felt."*

"Shelly, sometimes it's hard for me to forget how much I hurt you last week when I was sarcastic about how your hair looked. I know you said you forgave me, but it really bothers me what I did. I just want you to know I still feel bad."

"David, we had a rough time yesterday shopping for a new backpack. I can still feel your anger at me for not allowing you to get the one you wanted. Would you be okay if we talked about it some more together? I would like to hear more about what you have to say."

To help express past regrets, I recommend bringing up past hurts from time to time so that your child or teenager believes that your 'self-discovery' is indeed, 'for real.' *"Michelle, I am so glad I came to know the truth about myself."*

Parents must remember not to protect their own ego or reputation when they are looking to establish emotional trust. When we model vulnerability, we set the conditions for our kids to see first hand the power of self-examination.

A mother of four came to realize that for years she has shown favoritism to her oldest son. After becoming aware of this, she decided to confront this truth head-on. The mom found a quiet place to talk where she knew there would be no distraction. She began by saying:

"David, I have a confession to make. May I tell you about it?" After hearing 'Yes', she continued. *"My heart is heavy because I have hurt you so much by spending so much time with your brother, Steven. I have ignored your needs and your heart. I haven't been there for you in the same ways I have been there for Steven. I can feel how much resentment you have for me. I have created feelings of jealousy in you. I hope in time you can forgive me. I am going to spend a lot more time with you from now on. This will never happen again! Is it okay that I tell you all this?"*

If you see your child is getting fatigued from this emotional moment, you might add, *"Let's continue talking about this later when you have more energy."* If they indicate they want to continue, then dive deep into more truth. This process is not a one-time event where our emotional history is forgiven in that moment. On the contrary, we must prove our way back each day.

Rule Three

"Serena, I know I mention this from time to time but I can't forget how wrong I was when I made you feel like you just use me for money or favors. It was me who ruined what we once had together. I am so thankful you told me. I know you can hear it in my voice and see it in my eyes."

TELLING CHILDREN ABOUT YOUR SPOUSE'S BEHAVIOR

Obviously if your spouse continues to remain defensive and tries to prevent you from saying the truth in front of you with your children present, it's best not to continue. The added stress on your children and on yourself, is not worth it. Still, you must never forfeit telling the truth in private to keep the peace. Besides, the peace will be short-lived. Try not to focus on your how your spouse will react if and when they find out. Do not live in fear. Your children's well-being comes first. *(See Difficult Spouse page 102).*

If you are married to a spouse who consistently is unable to confront hard truths about themselves, you are left with no choice but to continue to talk in private to your children about what is not normal so they can get relief as well as not develop a penchant for alternative realities. The trick is not to go past what they experience and poison their love for that parent. Having the strength to say the truth to your children with a caring tone is essential to their long term well- being.

Talking with a culture of truth does not demean Mom or Dad. It simply acknowledges the truth. *"Alicia, I know you know how much your mother loves you, but she struggles with knowing how to express her emotions. Sometimes she can be cold for no reason. It's not your fault. It is a terrible feeling the way Mom makes you feel when she blames you. She needs professional help. Sometimes she is ready to get help and sometimes she is not. I know you have lots of questions. Let's keep talking about it."*

"David, I'm sorry you had to hear your father speak to me sarcastically in the car today. I know it upsets you when he becomes a bully. The truth is, Dad has difficulty controlling his moods."

Children, like any adult, can handle multiple emotions as long as they learn how to separate truth from forced loyalty. We can be upset or scared, and still have feelings of connection.

"Jeremy, I saw how dad made you feel when he came in your room. You were reading and just doing your work, and he started yelling. Even though he loves you so much, he really has trouble with his moods. I will tell your father tonight the way he makes you feel."

"Michelle, Mommy and I have been arguing too much lately and to help her calm down, sometimes I sleep in another room. I know you know that sometimes Mommy has trouble controlling her moods. I love mommy very much and I know you do too. Never be afraid to tell me how you feel. In our family we can talk about anything."

Although talking this way will not take away the child's bad feelings away caused by the unaware parent, it will ground the child not to deny what they see and feel. This is no small matter! We never want our children to lose their confidence and instincts about what they see, hear and feel. Our instincts are a vital self-guiding force in making good decisions, including who to be friends with, and one day, who to marry.

Of course, truth must be tempered with the wisdom of age-appropriateness and common sense. A father who finds himself sleeping on the couch after fighting with his wife does not want to tell his five-year-old son or daughter, "I'm teaching Mommy a lesson."

If you stay the course in communicating this vital relationship rule, one day your spouse will know the truth about their own behavior directly from their children. Nothing is more sobering than when our children tell us how we make them feel. It can motivate any parent to say, "Enough, it's time for me to get help and change!"

Rule Three

FAMILY LOYALTY VS. THE TRUTH

It is a false choice to draw a distinction between family loyalty and speaking the truth. It really isn't that hard to love someone and at the same time, call out the truth. I have seen these false choices tear families apart more than politics. How many of us know a family member who rarely speaks, or perhaps not at all, to a brother, sister, uncle, even a parent, because that family member won't acknowledge the truth about past experiences or current behaviors. A brother is always giving unwanted advice to his sister's husband, making him feel; "You're a nice guy, but not too smart." A sister talks to her brother's wife in a selfish way because she's a know-it-all." A mother is always lecturing her new daughter-in-law on how to run a kitchen. A father's sarcasm to his own married son has become too much for his wife to bear. As a result, if they do visit a family member, they keep their visits short and superficial.

We can be loyal and show love at the same time as long as we say things, at least in private, to our spouse who craves to hear the truth. *"Honey, we both know your mother can be moody and show favoritism."* Standing on the side of the truth, even if it goes against the bruised ego of a mother, brother, a sister, a father, mother or spouse, is the signature of maturity and living with a culture of truth.

FAMILY MENTAL HEALTH ISSUES

It's surprising how many parents avoid telling their children about their own family members (spouse, grandma, grandpa, aunts, uncles, brothers and sisters) who may have serious psychological issues such as depression, severe anxiety, bipolar disorder, or maybe a form of ASD (Autistic Spectrum Disorder) to name just a few *(The Difficult Spouse p.102).*

We should talk openly and regularly about mental health issues; it should be discussed with the highest degree of respect and emotional caring. It's not as important to name the diagnosis, as much as it is to be able to talk about the behaviors.

At the same time we need to acknowledge how those behaviors makes your child or teenager feel. This is hardly a one-time conversation. This kind of dialogue should continue throughout their full development and well beyond. Some parents fear that if they acknowledge such problems, they may discover that they have some of the same issues, or by bringing these issues to light, may cause their children to behave in similar ways. They won't. Children who are given the truth as soon as they are able to understand it, will become inoculated on several fronts. First, they will not grow up with the feeling, "It must be my fault that I am treated this way." Second, later in life they will be better at spotting disturbed behaviors in others. Not educating children about abnormal behaviors has serious unintended consequences, including the risk of being drawn into future dysfunctional relationships themselves. Having the strength to face the truth about those we love, is essential to remaining emotionally healthy.

Too many family members come together only in crisis, insisting that they really have each other's back. While that may be true, what they don't have are each other's hearts. When we don't feel safe to express our truest feelings, we begin building a fortified steel bunker around our weakness so we can hide out. We learn quickly how unsafe it is to be honest and vulnerable. We begin carrying too many secrets behind our eyes.

As a consequence we become more of a stranger to ourselves, unsure and often numb to how we feel. Later in life we wind up sitting with a therapist and revealing, "I'm not even sure who I am anymore." As a result of living in a culture of truth, your home will be filled with more than just great food, it will be filled with more laughter and more self-awareness.

> Having the strength to face the truth about those we love, is essential to remaining emotionally healthy

Rule Three

EXPRESSIONS THAT MODEL A CULTURE OF TRUTH

"What's happening between us that you did not want me to know?"

Puts the emphasis on the relationship, not the disappointment.

"In our family..."

Use it when your child invokes comparisons, i.e.,"But Bobby's parents allow it." or, "All my other friends have a cell phone now, why can't I?" Or, use it as a learning moment when you see other kids or adults behaving poorly. *"Robert, you see that boy over there. Wow! Look at how he is pushing his mother. In our family, we never push. I know you know that."*

    This expression will become one of those wonderful phrases that can never be said too many times. It reinforces a child's secure base, establishing predictability. It also reinforces the child's family values and differences between other families.

"Good or No Good?"

This simple expression helps young children know themselves better and gets you the bottomline faster. It puts the focus on personal preferences: *"How do you like this park—good or no good?" "How did you like the sandwich—good or no good?"* Make this expression a theme for years.

"Thanks for reminding me."

Parents should say this in front of their children when their own negative behavior is brought to their attention. The expression, *"Thanks for reminding me"* creates a non-defensive relaxed atmosphere. Teach your children to say it back to you, when you remind them of something negative they do too.

"True or not true?"

This is a great follow-up expression that reinforces personal truthfulness. *"Sam, you keep grabbing the Lego pieces out of your brother's hand. True or not true?"* If the child says *not true*, you say, *"I know you know it's true."* Don't debate with him. If he says, *True,* say, *"I knew you knew the truth. That's one of the qualities I respect so much about you, your honesty."* Make this expression a theme for years.

Rule Four

ENFORCE CONSEQUENCES CONSISTENTLY

SELF-CONTROL

> *Rules without relationship leads to rebellion.*
> —JOSH MCDOWELL

Of all the five rules, parents struggle the most with *Rule Four*. They struggle primarily in three ways: *not following through consistently, showing anger or upset too quickly and not knowing which consequence fits what situation.*

Most parents live with their children from moment to moment, exacting obedience or excusing disobedience on impulse rather than on principle. Screen-time is over in three minutes, no more snacks in the car, have the car back by 9 p.m., bedtime is 8:30, dinner in five minutes. When you enforce consequences consistently, you teach about the laws of nature, the laws of man, and, of course, the laws above us all. Enforcing consequences consistently leads to the life skill of *self-control*. Self-control also leads to greater happiness and self-respect.

Unenforced consequences cause increased anxiety as a result of not knowing when or where the hammer of discipline will fall. The child will come to think, "I know I broke the rule," and becomes anxious wondering if and when the consequence will arrive. Most times it doesn't. I'm *not* an advocate of warnings or three-strikes and you're out. I'm an advocate of one-strike and you're out. *Setting limits without enforcement is*

> Unenforced consequences cause increased anxiety as a result of not knowing when or where the hammer of discipline will fall

not discipline, it's confusion. That's why parents must think twice before setting a limit or rule. "Does it fit the situation? And more importantly, can I enforce it?" No sense in saying, "The next time you do that we're leaving," if in fact you are unable to leave. Your kids must come to *really* believe you mean what you say and say what you mean, all without "being mean."

There is a big difference between tough love and tough parenting. There is, however, one caveat. If your relationship is fractured and in need of repair, postpone your consequences temporarily and focus on the other four rules. *(See The Difficult Child, page 129.)* This is why I have placed this rule much later in the book. It is worth repeating: *Rules without relationship lead to rebellion.*

BE THE REF BUT STAY CALM

I cannot over-emphasize the importance of controlling your temper when you enforce a consequence. If you don't, you diminish your child's motivation to examine their own behavior and instead you'll draw them closer to your own drama. To help stay calm, think of yourself as a professional referee making a call. When a referee makes a tough call on the playing field, it's never personal. They stick to the rules, give the penalty, and avoid being drawn into the individual drama in the moment. Parents need to do the same thing with their children; call out the behavior, and give the consequence, with respect, calmness and confidence.

"Ben, I saw you push your brother out of the way to make

sure you got to sit 'shotgun.' Not only will your brother Alex sit up front now, but for the next two times when we take the car as well. I know you know the truth Ben and I respect you for it." Reject only the negative behavior, never the child. The more a child trusts you emotionally (Rule One), the more they will accept what you have to say or do.

"Ellen, when you get into a bad mood, you go too far in how you talk and behave. You roll your eyes and become sarcastic. It's not the best of you." Then pause for ten-seconds and lay down the consequence. "I know you are not surprised that we won't be going out now." That ten-second calm delay, before laying down the consequence makes a huge difference.

Never match your child's intensity, especially if your child is already high-strung and wound tight. If your children are not used to being held responsible for their behaviors, you can expect boos, hisses and complaints: "It's not fair." "You're mean." "It wasn't me." *A word of caution: be 110% sure that you are right before you make the call.* If you are wrong, you will lose trust. The child will think, "You really don't know me." Never take the risk if you are not 110% on the money. If in doubt, leave it out! Wait for another time. I promise, it's right around the corner.

Some who are reading this now might ask: When we become the *ref*, who's to say who has the *truth*? There's my truth, then there's your truth. It seems everyone will claim a different truth. Yes, sometimes it's true that there are multiple ways of seeing the truth. But others who are reading this know exactly what I mean when I say that in the context of emotional conflict, there's really only one truth about what really happened and why. It is a question of to what degree a parent is willing to model openness and patience in order to arrive at what really happened during or before a moment of conflict. The main benefit of staying calm is that it allows your child to focus on *their* misbehavior, rather than on *your* upset.

Imagine being pulled over by a policeman for running a red light. Instead of the officer remaining calm and respectful, he was aggressive, rude and insulting. "Are you crazy? You could have hit someone! You're a lousy driver! Give me your license and registration right now." In all likelihood, under those circumstances you would have driven off cursing the officer and thinking, "What a loudmouth! What a jerk!" You would have been hell bent on blaming the cop for your ticket and not yourself. Children will respond in the same way.

Parents should also refrain from sounding like all hope is lost. "That's it! You're grounded until I say so." Or, "You can't use the car or your cell phone until I can trust you again." The danger is that children and teenagers are very capable of losing their motivation to earn back a privilege when you make them feel hopeless. As a result, they learn only how to "do the time." Better to say, *"You can begin earning back your cell phone when you complete all your homework for one week. I have no doubt you can successfully do that."* Be clear upfront how long your consequence will stay in effect. They need to consistently feel your unrelenting optimism and deep belief in their potential (see *Rule Five*).

When Zack started screaming at his sister, his mother remained calm, serious and respectful saying: *"Zack, when you scream at your sister, it drains my energy and generosity. Because of this, I'm no longer willing to drive you to the park. I know you understand. I also know you can control yourself completely. Zack, I am going to the kitchen now. When you're back in control, you will find me there and I want to hear everything you want me to know."* Then, walk out of the room calmly, separating yourself from his tantrum.

Although this example may sound like a formal way to speak, it highlights your self-control, respect and consistency. The real learning power of delivering a consequence comes from doing so in an unceremonious way. To that end, the child has to see there's no longer a big response to his negativity, only a quiet result, and all

> You never win cooperation on the strength of your arguments, you win on the strength of your relationship

with respect. You never win cooperation on the strength of your arguments, you win on the strength of your relationship.

Finally, don't forget to show appreciation when your child does complete his/her consequence successfully, or, just as importantly, abided by your limit in the first place. "Zack, thank you for accepting that we're not going to the park now and playing on the swings. You accepted it like a man. I have such respect for you." Or, *"Chloe, thank you for accepting my decision to not let you go on the sleep-over this weekend. I have tremendous respect for your self-control. I know how bummed out you are." I really appreciate it."*

THE THREE MAIN CONSEQUENCES

It's no secret that parents would love to have a printed list of what the consequences should be for every behavior. Well, so far there is no list and for good reason. Certain types of consequences can wear off or backfire over time. It also helps to understand your child's temperament when determining which consequence you want to use. Temperament refers to inborn traits, such as being easygoing, flexible, intense, very active or slow to warm up. What works for one child, may not work for another.

To help parents understand what consequence fits what crime, it helps to understand the three most common types of consequences. They are: *the natural, the logical, and the unrelated consequence.* In the end, the natural and logical consequences are our best teachers in the long run.

1. THE NATURAL CONSEQUENCE

Natural consequences occur by themselves. They are not controlled or manipulated by anyone. For example, if a child jumps into a puddle, his shoes will get wet. Or if a child refuses to eat his lunch at school, he will be more hungry at dinner. When a child doesn't want to bring a warmer coat with him on a cold day, the natural consequence of being cold teaches the lesson. It's that simple and natural! There is no need to rub your child's nose in his poor decision-making or stubbornness.

"See Robert, I told you to take the warmer coat!"

I can assure you Robert will know that himself next time. Leave room for dignity. Depending on the situation, parents often worry that natural consequences can be too harsh and [they] are unwilling to tolerate their children's discomfort or unhappiness, so they intervene too early.

Sabotaging a natural consequence by rescuing the child too soon denies the power of the obvious lesson. Examples include: continually bringing a forgotten backpack to school or paying for a teen's excessive cell phone bill. When 11-year-old Marvin, who always forgets to take his homework to school, calls his mom one morning to bring him his book report, his mother shows concern, but does not rescue him. *"It's tough being the only one in class without your homework. You worked hard on it. You can take it tomorrow, but for today you will probably get a lower grade. I know you understand, Marvin."*

While natural consequences remain a powerful motivator for the child to think ahead, parents should exercise common sense before applying a natural consequence. Obviously, if your child is struggling in school or perhaps has a learning difference, it would be unwise not to support your child by helping him keep up in class. Tutors, other special resources, or even a change of schools should be a part of the solution.

2. THE LOGICAL CONSEQUENCE

The logical consequence is also called, 'the take-away'. They can include privileges such as, cell phones, electronics, bicycles, everything really. One thing to remember about take-aways, is that if children don't feel the loss, they probably won't learn the lesson.

It is much easier for a child to make the connection between leaving a bike outside in the rain and not being allowed to ride it the following day, than it would be for him to make the connection between leaving the bike outside and an unrelated consequence like not going on a field trip. Remember, remain calm and respectful.

1. *Have a child clean up an art mess he deliberately made* before being allowed to work on another project. From this children will learn, "I can fix things when I mess up."
2. Not wearing s*eat belts.* Here's a tough but very effective consequence for teenagers who won't wear their seat belts regularly. Each time you are with them, add an additional day past the day they can take their driver's permit test. Rarely do teenagers want to lose even a single day.
3. Not *cleaning up the dog poop in the yard.* Try having your son or daughter run through the yard barefoot! Watch the yard get picked up just right and on time. The child of course should be at least 12 years of age.

3. THE UNRELATED CONSEQUENCE

Finally there are unrelated consequences. These are consequences that may not be directly related to a child's behavior but are, instead, devised by an adult as a way to get the child to regret what they did. Most unrelated consequences involve losing a privilege or being penalized. They are also known as "take-aways."

Earlier bedtime. For each infraction, according to your child's behavior that day, he will be told to go to bed five minutes earlier.

Take away Cell Phone. If your teenager isn't doing his or her homework, take away his cell phone. Usually, a 24 hour loss of privileges will do the job.

Take Door Off Hinges. If your teenager is defiantly closing or locking the door to his room to keep you or other family members out, or each time you open the door to your child's room you catch him in a continued act of disobedience, here's a suggestion: Take your child's door off the hinges until he earns back the right to a closed door. It sounds harder to do than it actually is. Yes, it works!

Pour Trash On Bed. If your child continues to eat or brings any food into the parents' bed, pour his small trash basket in his room onto his bed. Do it calmly without anger and say; "I know you prefer your bed to be clean, so do I."

If unrelated consequences are chosen as a discipline strategy, it is best to make the consequence something about which the child can be positively recognized later for his or her effort to make it right. Like having the child vacuum the living room, or clean out a portion of the garage, as opposed to being asked to sit in their room and think about what they did wrong. In this way, work will get done, and the child will feel a sense of satisfaction and accomplishment.

TAKE A TIME BREAK - A DIFFERENT WAY TO EXPRESS AN OLD IDEA

Its predecessor, "time-out," is an overused expression that carries with it childish feelings. Also, the words "time-out" places the focus on the word "*out*," which in itself triggers a contest of wills when children hear it. Specifically, the word 'out' is taken as banishment, rejection and a threat to the relationship. It is heard as, "Get out and stay out!" The expression *Time Break* is more than just a change of words, it is a change in attitude. The word 'break' is heard very differently. We all need a break now and then.

Rehearse this consequence with your children after you introduce them to it. *"Jason, let's practice this new consequence together. Let's pretend that I just heard you use a disgusting word. Then I will say: 'disgusting word'— take a 'time break.'*

> Specifically, the word 'out' is taken as banishment, rejection and a threat to the relationship. It is heard as, "Get out and stay out!

You can walk to another room or you can stand there until you are back in control. Practice going through the motions, so that his brain will have a memory map of what to do and where to go. You might also suggest having him come up with his own 'time break space'— with a big pillow, a comfortable chair or a room with a few favorite books.

How long your child stays in the 'time break' is not nearly as important as completing it successfully. Don't forget to express appreciation when they do complete it. *"Emily, you really handled that 'time break' well! You could have kicked and screamed more, but you controlled yourself. You did it successfully. Thank you!"* Depending on your child's temperament, it only has to be 10 seconds, 30 seconds, a minute, or 10 minutes. Each amount of time will serve the purpose perfectly. You may think that such a short break is no consequence at all, but it is. The reinforcement of your child's successful effort, and your refusal to get caught up in his emotional drama is what will change his future behavior. Do not be persuaded when your child tells you how "stupid" 'time breaks' are. Look serious, but not angry. Reinforce how well they are back in control of themselves. Do not get drawn into a debate. It is a battle you cannot win. Taking a 'time break' for a broken rule or limit can happen as frequently as needed.

Another way to effectively teach the 'time break' is to announce out loud that you (the parent) need a time break yourself. This also reinforces the consequence as a natural part of exercising self-control. For example, *"Michael, I'm feeling very angry right now. I need a 'time break'. I'm going into the living room to take a few minutes to calm myself down. When I feel more in control, I will return."*

I suggest you announce where you're going rather than just walk away. It shows respect, and communicates that you are not emotionally trying to get away from your child. I also suggest to re-enter the room a few moments later. Let your child see how quickly you can recover and calm down— about two minutes is best.

THE BROKEN RECORD

One of the most effective ways to stop being drawn into a debate while maintaining limits with very young children (not teenagers), is called *The Broken Record*. Simply put, you keep repeating the same information over and over (with patience and heart), as if you were a broken record.

The key is to repeat this with calmness, brevity and total respect (*Rule Two*). Do not sound uncaring, impatient or robotic. Initially this process can take anywhere from three minutes to 30 minutes. Do not be drawn into any level of debate. Practice this properly and you will forever change the outcome of potential meltdowns with very young children.

> **Parent:** *"I know you'd like to stay up. It's 8:30 and time for you to be in your bed."*
>
> **Child:** *"Just five more minutes."*
>
> **Parent:** *"I know you'd like to stay up. It's time for you to be in your bed.*

Child: *"I'm not tired."*

Parent: *"I see that. It's 8:30 and time for you to be in your bed."*

Child: *"Why do you keep repeating the same thing?"*

Parent: *"You don't like that I keep telling you what you already know. But it is 8:30 and time for bed. I know you know it."*

Obviously if you're in public, it is best to leave and find a private place to allow your child to continue to carry on. If you can prove to your child you will not give in, and at the same time not detach, you will have passed a crucial milestone. Allowing a child to cry, whine, or complain for as long as he likes without losing your cool and respect will, over time, create that tipping point for change. By reacting in these counter-intuitive ways, you are reinforcing emotional trust.

Again, the secret is to ignore obnoxious behaviors without ignoring the child. *"Justin, you can take as long as you want to remain upset. I know this is not easy for you to accept."* Maintain a high level of *empathy* (Rule One) and *respect* (Rule Two) during these stress points. Do not become embarrassed by other adult reactions. Years from now, you will have the kind of relationship with your children other parents would give anything to have.

While all children must learn how to master their emotions, it comes as no surprise that we seem to discriminate more against boys than girls when it comes to our expectations about controlling moods and tempers. We seem to allow girls much more slack as they cycle through their emotions. It is as if we say, "You're a girl and you can't help it." Putting aside the obvious hormonal issues that trigger the physical changes of puberty, girls are more than capable of keeping their moods in check if they are taught how. This kind of private conversation should start at about ten years of age. In a relaxed way, begin to explain how moods can sometimes seem to appear from nowhere.

"Deanna, I know that sometimes a sudden feeling of sadness

or anger can come over you fast. It's confusing." Let your daughter weigh in on this. She will. Create the feeling of an open and relaxed conversation. *"Joanie, that bad mood that is coming over you now, you can push it back. You will feel better right away. Don't let it take you over."*

What a huge difference this will make in your daughter's life. The first reason is that she will not feel helpless, thinking, *I must suffer through these episodes of ups and downs because I have no control.* Second, other family members won't feel resentful about being subjected to those changing mood cycles.

AVOID THE WORD 'PUNISHMENT'

I want to underscore the psychological importance of *not* using the word *punishment* when we enforce a consequence. As a practical matter, a consequence and a punishment seem to mean the same thing. Still, the word *punishment* serves as a trigger and makes children focus on their anger toward their parents, rather than on their own behaviors. Swapping out those words will help shift the focus away from the parent as the enforcer back to the child or teenager who blew past the limit. It's subtle, but it works. There is a world of difference when a parent says, "The consequence is staying home for the afternoon" versus, "Your punishment is staying home all afternoon."

That simple change in language allows the child to focus much more on what they did, so you become less of a target for retaliation and resentment. In the end, you can't punish kids into acceptable behavior. Research shows that children become more moral and more able to "do right" when they're raised without the feeling of always being *punished*. It may sound pedantic but the word *punishment* adds an overlay of shame and guilt that typically will only make children rebel more.

NO CONSEQUENCES FOR NAGGING AND WHINING

It is worth repeating that you should not set a time limit on how long you allow your child to whine, complain or nag. There should be no consequences for whining. Naturally, it's disturbing to listen. It's easy to become angry fast. "Justin, act like a big boy. Quit crying already!" "I'm going to ignore you if you keep nagging me!" This is an ideal window to model patience and empathy. The key is not to appear angry, detached or uncaring during these episodes.

Your child will continue to test you, to see if you will break your calm ways. *"Justin, I know you don't like me now for not giving you what you want. It hurts me too when I see how upset you are, but I respect you too much to give in to you. I know you can control yourself. You can stay upset for as long as you like and I will understand. "Yes, your child will continue for a bit but sooner than you think your child will come to the realization,* Wow, I can control myself.

Another way to handle temper tantrums with young children is to switch locations. Simply say, "You can continue your upset in the backyard. When you're finished, come back inside so we can be together." Sometimes, when there isn't an audience, the excitement of throwing a tantrum is gone.

STOP SAYING THE WORD 'NO'

Twenty years ago I wrote an entire book on this one word, *When No Gets You Nowhere! Random House 1997.* The one exception to saying the word 'no' is when you are laying out a rule. Studies show that hearing rules in the negative, helps kids remember them.

"No running in the store." "No slamming the car door." "No using bad words."

Apart from that exception, avoid the word entirely. Young children will hear the word 'no' over 200 times a day from teachers, parents, grandparents, almost everyone. The word automatically triggers conflict. When kids make a request that either you can't do, won't do or won't allow, just present the facts. Do not say the word "no" in your answer. *"Danny, I wish I could take you. Unfortunately, I have to leave now for my office for a business appointment."*

"Alicia, the toy is something I do not have the money for today. I wish I did." Keep the reason simple. No more than five-seconds. Stay elegant and respectful with heartfelt regret regarding why you are unable to do what your child wants. Do not be drawn into debate. Your child will quickly come to the conclusion that what they want, is not happening! If your child keeps nagging, use the *The Broken Record* strategy *(see page 98)*. It's not how fast you can get a child to stop, but how fast you can get him to think! Here are the main reasons for eliminating the word "no:"

- *Allows the child the time to think and reason.*
- *Shows respect for the child's ability to figure things out.*
- *Does not make the parent the messenger of the word "no."*
- *Takes the focus away from the parent just giving out arbitrary "no's."*

HOW TO ENFORCE CONSEQUENCES

KEEP YOUR MELODY HUMBLE

Never enforce a consequence with anger or sarcasm. It sets up a challenge. As you put *Rule Four* into action, it's worth repeating that *a*lthough our words are super important, they are not nearly as important as our tone of voice, facial expressions and body language. We must always control *our melody* if we *want* to build trust, excite understanding and project respect. For example, you can say with real warmth, *"Daniel, we talked* about your back-talk to me earlier. I have too much respect for you and for myself to ignore what you said to me. As of now you will not be going to Marty's house after school tomorrow. I know you have respect for my decision."

BE CONSISTENT

Mean what you say and say what you mean, but never sound mean. Be predictable.

BE SPECIFIC WHEN YOU SET LIMITS

Children and teenagers respond better to limit-setting when parents give detailed rather than abstract information. Eight-year-old Nathan will respond better to, *"In five minutes it's time to leave"* rather than, "Soon, it will be time to leave."If a parent says, "David, you can only stay on the Internet a little while longer," David will see this as an invitation to test the limit. Does "little" mean 10 minutes or 30 minutes? Better to say, *"David, you can use the Internet for three more minutes."*

Although he will likely still try to push through the three-minute limit, he will not be confused about what the limit was when you enforce the consequence. You will be unpopular, but you will not be unfair. Eight-year-old Nathan will respond better to, *"In five-minutes it's bed time"* than, "Soon it's time to go to bed." Takeaway: Give concrete information rather than talking in the abstract.

WHEN YOU MAKE A REQUEST, ASK ONLY ONCE

If your child does not follow your instructions, provide a consequence. This is called *"the one request."* No warning, no negotiations, no threats, and no reiteration of the rule—just a quiet consequence. Resist the temptation to repeat the request, or to worry about whether your child actually heard you. Children learn best when actions and consequences are closely linked in time and are without fanfare. The more you talk and explain, the more you diminish your effectiveness. Do not threaten with statements like, "If you do that again I'm going to take away another hour of screen time." Or, "I'm not kidding this time." Children learn two things from a quick and unceremonious consequence:

Lesson 1: The child will get a predictable outcome, which is the ultimate deterrent. It also lowers their anxiety level.

Lesson 2: They learn you will not argue, debate or reiterate a rule.

If for practical reasons you can't enforce the consequence in that moment or you are not sure what consequence should be enforced, it is not the end of the world, as long as these moments are the exception. A delayed consequence linked to the behavior later will still work. Refuse to get drawn into matching your child's negative energy with smirks, sarcasm, loudness or other disrespectful behaviors. Remember, the goal is to change behavior, not the child. Another way to understand this is: Tough love is not tough parenting!

Children will come to know you mean what you say, and you say what you mean. The key is to remain caring (empathic) and respectful as you follow through. *"Asher, I know you know you're a half-hour late with the car. You know I meant it when I said 9:30. As a result, you will not have the car for one week. I know you respect me for holding you to your word the way I respect you."* This may seem like a formal way to talk, but I can assure you it will underscore an enormous tone of respect.

EXPRESS APPRECIATION AT COMPLETION

Do not remain silent after a consequence is completed successfully. Instead, immediately express honest appreciation in a relaxed and low-key way.

"Adam, you could have fought me when I asked you to go to your room, but you didn't. You went there and controlled yourself. I really appreciate that. I know you felt good about it too! Thank you."

The same principle holds true when your child listens the first time. Don't ignore compliance. *"Thank you, Brian, for turning off your music when I asked."* Doing this will bring higher levels of cooperation.

"Justin, you were thinking about calling your sister a name, but you didn't. You were successful in controlling your temper."

"Sarah, I really appreciate the way you did not fight back when I asked you to log off the Internet."

HOUSE RULES

If all we do as parents is remain rigid and tell children what they can't do, rebellion isn't a matter of *if*, it's just a matter of *when*. This is why the fewer house rules we have, the more effectively the ones we do have will work.

1. **No Yelling** (screaming room-to-room, etc.)
2. **No Hitting** (hands, feet, body, head, kicking, biting)
3. **No Disrespect** (faces, teasing, eye-rolling, slamming doors, back-talk)
4. **No Tattling** (unless someone is hurt or about to get hurt)

HOW TO INTRODUCE THE HOUSE RULES

Ideally, both parents should present the rules together, each one giving over two rules. Obviously, single parents can do this easily by themselves as well. Also, try to refrain from using the word 'meeting' when you call your kids together. The word 'meeting' is a business term and conjures up tension, performance and anxiety. The words 'discussion' or 'conversation' sets the proper tone and context for how you envision all family conversations.

When your children all arrive in the kitchen, not the living room, use each of their names before you begin, *"Alex, Maya, and David....Mom and I have something important we want to say to all of you. Lately, there has been a lot of yelling, name-calling and pushing in our family. We all want the good times to happen more and we want to get rid of all that yelling and fighting. The truth is Mom and I have ignored these rules too long. That's going to change. Starting right now we are all going to live by four simple house rules."*

When you present the house rules, start with the word "no," Starting right now there will be *"No disrespect," "No tattling," "No yelling,"* and *"No hitting."* This is counter to what we have always been taught about saying things only in the 'positive'. It is easier for children to grasp the meaning of a rule faster when you state it in the negative.

After describing in detail what each behavior means, encourage a family discussion around them. *"That's right, Alex, hitting includes our feet and even our bodies when we push." "Maya, what do you think about what Alex said?"* At the end, ask each child to repeat back one rule and explain what it means to them. Try to wait until one of your children asks, *"What will happen if we break a rule?"* You can respond, *"Maya, excellent question! If you break the rule, I will immediately tell you which one you broke."*

For example, *"Maya, the rule in our house is no yelling at each other. I know you know that. Just talk to your brother calmly and he will come around."* Other times I will ask you to take a *'time break' (see p. 96)* and ask you to come back when you are in control again." Explain that if she does not go on her own, you will walk her there, or you will pick her up and take her.

It's okay if your kids are restless and slouching during the talk. It's more important that they take in the information, than they sit up straight in their chairs. Let them be animated. At the conclusion of your family conversation you will want to say (include in your prepared notes), *"We know you each understand the rules now, and we have no doubt you will be successful in maintaining them."*

A WORD ABOUT TATTLETALE BEHAVIOR

No doubt your children will want to talk about tattling in the family. Spend about five minutes on tattling and give different examples. For example, you may ask, "If you know that there is no eating in the living room and you see Jacob eating there, should you tell us?" Ask your children to come up with their own examples as well. "Michelle, please go upstairs and tell me if Justin is watching TV?" Or Ellen,"see if Michael has started his homework." *Do not train your children to be detectives or spy on your behalf.* Parents should teach what stand-up behavior is. No one likes a snitch.

Explain that they should *only* "tell" if someone is hurt, or is about to get hurt. Let them know this rule should apply at school too. Ask: "What does it mean when someone is hurt or about to get hurt?" Give examples. Engage in lively conversation about what this means. Be prepared for children to be overly dramatic. Some kids can get pretty gruesome. Allow it. Remain calm and let the process work its way through to the practical. Tell your children to always let you, or any adult, know when someone is hurt or about to get hurt. Tell your children you are confident they know the difference between an emergency and silly behavior. Continue talking about it.

Like everything, your kids will test you. When your child does tell you about their brother or sister doing something they shouldn't, you can respond with: *"Justin, remember our family rule: No tattling! And remember, no one can tattle on you either!"* When your child has fully absorbed the concept of tattling, bring up one last time, the one exception: "Only if someone is hurt or about to get hurt. If that is happening, always come to us!"

PREPARATION

The Place:

Have it in the kitchen or family room.

What To Bring:

I suggest bringing in a paper notepad (*definitely not a digital notebook*) to take notes and to read from it if you need to. No need to memorize. It should include some of the ideas you're reading here as well as other parenting ideas you may have. Also, let them know that what they say is important and you may write down some of their ideas so you can remember them for later. It signals to your children that you take what they are saying very seriously.

Few children have ever experienced an adult writing down what they say. It shows tremendous respect! Remain super relaxed with a positive attitude. This leaves children with an optimistic feeling that everything is going to work out. Having both parents participate reinforces the message that, "My parents are in complete agreement."

How Long:

The whole discussion should not take more than about 10 minutes.

Rule Five

SHOW UNRELENTING OPTIMISM
▼
SELF-CONFIDENCE

*Positive energy makes you feel that
something great is always about to happen.*
—MARK L. BRENNER

Our fifth and final parenting rule fulfills our last relationship need — *believe in me*. Rule Five builds self-confidence.

For children, experiencing your calmness and unrelenting positive attitude is proof you believe in them. After all, if you are calm and positive, you must really believe they can do what is in front of them, even though in that moment he or she may not. It consistently allows a child who hesitates for a moment to see a different outcome. *"David, I was just thinking of all the ways I trust you. I know when I leave the house, everything will be okay."* Parents say they are positive, but their tone of voice and attitude may say differently.

What a gift to grow up in a house and feel believed in. Not just sometimes, or even most times— but all times. Parents can often see qualities in children that

> Without the skillful help of an optimistic and patient adult, most children and teenagers remain trapped in their struggles

their children can't see in themselves. Without the skillful help of an optimistic and patient adult, most children and teenagers remain trapped in their struggles. The Talmud, the comprehensive body of Jewish law and philosophy, says: "The prisoner cannot free himself from prison." We all need the continued support and belief of a charismatic person to break free from self-doubt.

Think of communicating unrelenting optimism as though you are quietly "willing" your child through a difficult moment. Three-year-old Leah is told, "I know you know where the spoon belongs," even though she is inclined not to put it back where it belongs. Ten year-old Stephen, who is about to go into a tantrum is told, "I can see you're figuring out how to control yourself."

> If all you ever talk about are problems, you have a problem relationship

Receiving positive emotional energy fuels our motivation to develop our talents and face our struggles. Communicating optimism makes us feel that something great is always about to happen. A wonderful quote by author, Dennis Mannering captures this spirit perfectly: Attitudes are contagious. Are yours worth catching? If all you ever talk about are problems, you have a problem relationship. *"Danny, I love the way you came into the kitchen just now. You look so happy and relaxed."* When children consistently sense our deep belief in them, cooperation and closeness soar. The secret sauce is the consistency. Optimism fuels self-confidence.

Having a sustained positive attitude and energy is not something that comes naturally for everyone. Just as there are physical takers in life, there are emotional takers too. As an experiment, the next time you are sitting with others, notice who puts out positive energy and who takes your energy. You may be surprised to see that it's not just the over-talkers or complainers, it can also be those who remain overly quiet, detached or bored. All these behaviors can be draining. You can always tell a positive and healing person in that you feel more energized after spending time with them.

Scientists tell us that our brains are wired to receive optimism which contributes to good health and a sustained feeling of well-being. It is why when we smile in a relaxed way, we can more easily influence others to cooperate. Positive and emotionally healthy people also help us feel good about ourselves. The Cloud isn't the only way to communicate wirelessly. The late Wayne Dyer reminds us, "You'll see it when you believe it." This new mindset will keep you focused, humble and energized.

> Receiving positive emotional energy fuels our motivation to develop our talents and face our struggles

The renowned child psychologist, Clark Moustakis elevated unrelenting optimism and faith above everything else.

> "Most importantly, there is faith. Not so much in the process (that is a given) but in the child! There is no clear-cut formula by which a parent conveys faith in a child. Faith is an intangible quality perceived largely through the presence of feelings, body language, and expressions. It is unspoken as much as it is spoken. It generates energy and inspiration and creates a feeling of well-being. When someone has faith in us, we are encouraged to face ourselves and express ourselves as the person we really are."

OPTIMISM IS A CHOICE

Much has been written on how to become a positive person. Daniel Goleman, the author of *Emotional Intelligence*, discovered the characteristics that produce optimism and positive energy more than 30 years ago. The most energetic people, he found, were "lively and engaged, extremely present, involved in the moment, often funny, yet profoundly at peace – even in disturbing situations." In other words, they're engaged in the here and now and not trapped in the past or preoccupied with the future. Optimists are open-minded and flexible.

An absurd joke helps us see this more clearly.

> *A fire broke out in a 40 story high rise. In order to save his own life, a man had to jump out the window. Another man on a much lower floor standing on the fire escape heard him saying on the way down, 'so far so good.'*

Iconic researcher, Dr. Paul Ekman, identifies four characteristics common to people with positive energy: First, a "palpable goodness" that goes far beyond some "warm and fuzzy aura" and seems to arise from genuine integrity. Second, an impression of selflessness—a lack of concern with status, fame, and ego—a "transparency between their personal and public lives." They are comfortable in their own skin with no need to prove their way into a person's life. Third, Ekman noticed they had a "compassionate physical and emotional energy when nurturing others."

And finally, the fourth quality included an "amazing power of attentiveness." They see, feel and and know just when to express what is happening. Some parents ask, "What if I'm not naturally an optimistic person?" Should I fake it and just act?" In a word, yes! Visualize what optimistic behavior looks like: walking with good posture, relaxed facial expressions, a great attitude, no sarcasm, no moodiness and generally communicating confidence that everything will workout. And, here's the metaphor. Great actors don't act, they behave. They behave in ways that the character would behave in, not in the ways they want to behave.

Remember, acting is really re-acting! As the legendary acting coach Sanford Meisner liked to say: " An ounce of behavior is worth a pound of words." In order to accomplish this magical transition, they visualize first exactly how their character would behave. If what they say or do does not fit the character, they drop it. Those mannerisms come through directly to those who are watching. I love this process because on the highest creative level, it allows for total transformation. Positive energy is not a loud force. We don't want to wake our kids up in the morning sounding like a cheerleader. "Good morning, rise and shine! What a great day!"

Everyone talks about renewable energy. Well, it's not surprising to learn that optimism is a renewable power source too. Staying positive will influence every aspect of your child's life, from wake time to sleep time. One caring mother, unaware of her negativity and anxiety answers the phone the same way with all her children: "Hi, everything okay?" This nervous question communicates doubt and worry. After all, anxious parents frequently have anxious children. A better way to communicate relaxed positivity would be: *"Hi, Emily, what's the good news?"* Even if your child is calling with bad news, you're letting her know your natural state of mind with her is not to worry. Optimism fuels hope, which in turn provides comfort, dignity and a deeper connection.

Here's an anonymous poem (with some of my own added stanzas) that highlights the vital need for communicating a positive deep belief in children:

A Boy in the Game

He stands at the plate, with heart pounding fast,
The bases are loaded, his focus must last.

Mom and Dad cannot help him, he stands all alone,
A hit right now would send the team home.

The ball crosses the plate, he swings and he misses,
There's a groan from the crowd, with some boos and some hisses.

A thoughtless coach's face expresses his doubt,
The boy looks away feeling lost in the count.

With confidence drained, his bat weighs a ton,
In that one moment, his swing is undone.
For it's moments like this, a man you can make,

Keep this in mind, when you guide a boy's fate.
And if you're not sure what this is about,
Think back to that "Coach," who triggered self-doubt.

Faces can be weapons, and hit hard like a fist,
These are the moments, we dare not miss.

THE HEAD COACH

Parents often ask, which parent should be the *head coach?* The answer, both.

The head coach of a healthy family doesn't walk around with a know-it-all attitude, sarcasm, moodiness, a lack of empathy or negative energy. The 11th century Rabbi and poet, Moshe Ibn Ezra said, "Words that come from the heart, enter the heart." You can't be a negative parent or a know-it-all and inspire trust, cooperation and optimism. To a large degree, the head coach relies on his/her positive energy to win the day.

As *head coach*, parents must also not elevate one child over another. Favoritism happens in the blink of an eye, especially when we are drawn to one child more easily because we relate to them more naturally and with less struggle. Siblings can feel it and carry that pain for years. Just as champion athletes bring out the best in each player on their team, the *head coach* knows how to help family members bring out the best in each other. They imagine themselves wearing a bold tee-shirt everyday that says: 'Team _____' (insert your family last name).

"Robert, just as I would not allow anyone in our family to make fun of you, I will not allow you to make fun of your sister. I know this is not the best of you. Nothing is more important to me, nothing, than the way we show respect to each other in our family. We will stay here together and talk it through until we all work it out together. And, I have no doubt we will."

Finally, as you lead your family in unity and victory, don't forget to laugh and have fun. Don't take yourself so seriously. Be multi-dimensional. The fun I'm talking about has little to do with going to cool places, or bribing kids with what they want just to win their affection. The fun I'm talking about is organic. Singing off key, telling a joke that doesn't work, looking silly, or just plain going along with the flow. It's been said that great parenting is somewhere between, *"Don't do that."* and *"Ah, what the hell."*

MOTIVATING YOUR CHILD

You can't make your child care just because you do. Some of the common mistakes parents make in trying to motivate their children include bribes, rewards, praise, threats, competitions, and punishments. These tactics in the long run work against both your child and your relationship. The qualities of true self-motivation demand freedom from outside evaluation. Parents often confuse motivation with giving praise. With praise, the take-away message is the parent's evaluation of the child's action or performance. Something is great, amazing, brilliant, disappointing. It becomes all about what the parent thinks. The challenge is to find creative ways that appeal to the individual nature of each child. For example, some kids are more motivated when they are awarded power, like being in charge of a project such as painting the walls in their room, or re-arranging the furniture in the family room or having them decide what restaurant or mall the family goes to, or having your son or daughter watch over a sibling when you have to go somewhere.

Five-year-old Michael is told before he leaves the house: *"Michael, let's go to Home Depot now. I'm looking to buy a new shower head. When we get to the store, let's both look for it. If I find it first, I'll pass it to you so you can put it in the cart."* Still other kids get motivated when they are paired with another child to do a *team project*. For them, teamwork will bring out their best and showcase their talents.

In an effort to motivate children, some parents believe that asking the question, "Can you do that?" sets up a positive challenge. Many believe that getting a commitment pushes the child to take an uncertain step. I believe the question alone communicates a lack of belief in the child. After all, if you have to ask, you must not know! Better to quietly say, *"Nate, I have no doubt in my mind you can do this."* Such a forward-looking expression allows a child to experience your unrelenting optimism and deep belief.

Rule Five

In contrast, when you express optimism, your attitude and positive energy (often without words) is what first comes through. You can see it through a warm smile, a gentle touch, an admiring nod or a thumbs-up.

Other tips to motivate include, eliminating using the word HELP almost completely. Remember, you are not the only one using this word. Teachers, extended family members, tutors all use this word everyday. Said *too* many times, makes a child feel helpless. Substitute the word PRACTICE. "Daniel, let's practice this together,", rather than... "Let me help you!" In addition, practice is an active word that everyone must do.

The word *practice* is far more motivating and builds an attitude of teamwork. So, the next time you want to say: *let me help you*, say: *"Let's practice."* It may sound grammatically incorrect, but it is psychologically sound! The word *practice* is far more motivating and builds an attitude of teamwork.

Finally, nine-year-old Kenny is told by his father, *"You can't control your little brother or anyone else in this family. You can only control yourself. You are only the boss of you. Your angry feelings will pass. You have the power to control your feelings. I know you know that."* Saying, *"I know you understand,"* or, *"I know you know that"* conveys three messages:

1. *You're telling him he has the intelligence to understand.*
2. *You show confidence in him to overcome the moment.*
3. *You are refusing to allow his own negativity to reinforce his negative self-image.*

Whatever your methods are to motivate, you should frame it in such a way that your child sees a positive glimpse of themselves into the future. Never threaten! Practice saying the words in the left column with a warm smile in your voice.

Positive		Negative
Danny, schoolwork first, then the Internet. You know that. Thank you.	**NOT**	If you don't do your homework, you don't go on the Internet.
Neil, finish helping your sister, then you can go to the backyard. Thanks!	**NOT**	If you don't finish helping, you can't go.
Claire, please help me put the groceries away, then you can take the car. Thanks!	**NOT**	If you don't help me, you can't go.

HOW TO EXPRESS UNRELENTING OPTIMISM

SHOW A CALM POSITIVE ENERGY

Show a quiet confidence of how we expect our children to behave. When they believe we really believe in them, they will yield. Yes, it is true. The secret is true believing. Children need a consistent feeling of optimism at home to sustain the enormous energy it takes to face their fears and overcome their challenges. Children (like adults), know when we fake it.

Optimists are open-minded and flexible. Optimists makes you feel that something great is always about to happen. Don't use negative phrases such as, "You can't," or "This won't work," and by all means don't complain about things which you have no control over.

RECOGNIZE ALL EFFORTS

"I noticed you put your backpack in your room as soon as you got home from school. Super."

"You made a full effort and you achieved a great result."

"You thought you couldn't do that, but you made a full effort anyway."

"Wow! You look pretty excited about the way you got that to work."

"You're working hard on that. No matter how hard, you keep at it!"

"You were frustrated, but you stayed with it."

"Look at how much you accomplished so far."

EXPRESS ENCOURAGEMENT, NOT PRAISE

A child learns of his competencies *not* from the parent praising how good he/she is at something, but by experiencing it for himself. Encouragement is a quiet psychological process that allows a child to go beyond a particular moment and see what is possible. *"I noticed you came into the kitchen so quietly right now... no running, no anger, and no demanding."* Praise on the other hand requires an outside judgment from others about how well something is done. "You do that great." "You're amazing."

Encouragement leaves the child with an opportunity to praise himself. It puts the focus on our internal motivation.

"You have what it takes to finish this hike."
"You can do it."
"You decide how to do that."
"Great discovery."
"Nothing can stop you now."
"You're catching on now."
"Bravo!" "You can handle this."
"You're on target."

SHOW AN UNRELENTING DEEP BELIEF

The late Wayne Dyer reminds us, "You'll see it when you believe it." Children need to hear at a minimum, five positive feedback comments for every negative feedback comment each day. "Sam, I love the way you helped your brother with his bicycle. You sure know how to be a friend."

One way to reinforce an unrelenting deep belief is to recall the details of past successes. The key is not to over-talk or over-sell it. It's a telling moment, not a selling moment.

THE POSITIVE / NEGATIVE RATIO

As a ratio, children need to hear at a minimum five positive encouraging comments for every negative one they hear each day. *"David, I love the way you organized your Legos™. You sure know how to be a friend."* It turns out that receiving unrelenting optimism fuels our vigor, determination and creativity.

Too often, we focus on telling our children what's wrong and forget to strengthen their strengths. This doesn't mean we should ignore obnoxious or stubborn behaviors, not at all. But when we continually point out too many mistakes or frown with disapproval, children begin to believe it's true and think, "This is who I am, what's the use!"

Parents need to create daily opportunities for children to feel, "I want to keep trying." We need to create a "try-again" culture. Even in our classrooms, too much emphasis today is placed on the dated model that gives a

Rule Five

child only one chance to test or one chance to do well at something. Although a teacher may provide multiple opportunities, their overall attitude may unwittingly convey, "This is it!"

A child's self-confidence will thrive when they have multiple chances to succeed and acquire the remarkable life quality we all admire—perseverance. After all, being a good test-taker is not nearly as valuable in life as the desire to keep trying. I am a strong supporter of Dr. William Glasser's pioneering work that led to his groundbreaking Quality School model. In his classrooms, when it comes time to test, books are opened, not closed! Research shows children will remember information longer when they are not forced to memorize for a test, but in a more relaxed way can look up the answer on the spot. Children learn that books are not to be feared with a memory test lurking behind every chapter. Instead, they are to be enjoyed with answers to be found at fingertips and now, more commonly, at keyboards. I encourage every school and educator to study and adopt this counter-intuitive model.

UNDERPERFORMING CHILDREN

Recognize that your child will have plateaus and setbacks. Do not remind him of his backsliding. When backsliding does occur, use expressions like, "It can happen. Next time, you'll do better." It is no secret that children who have low self-worth have a tendency not to work to their potential. They may be doing poorly in school, not because they are lazy, but because they have issues around success. Many would rather have the reputation of quitting rather than face the risk failing or falling behind.

If your child struggles on a daily basis to finish his or her homework, take a long-term view. Just take a break and say, *"Well, Jonathan, you completed one page of reading and two math problems. Well done! Let's take a break."* Although that amount of work is ridiculously small, show respect for it. Resist any temptation to be sarcastic or look disappointed. Do not be influenced by well-meaning educators, friends, or

> Children and teenagers who continually underperform do not have a lack of will; they have a lack of success

mental-health professionals who insist your child needs to learn the hard way.

A child who is really struggling to keep up is not faking it. In most instances, he or she can do it, but only with the right support—free from humiliation and threats. A struggling child who is threatened will translate the threat as, "You don't believe in me." In these cases, you should do everything you can to be sure your child does not fall behind, even If that means having to read the chapters to your child while he listens, or writing out his math problems, or keeping him organized — I strongly suggest you do it all. And by all means, coordinate with his teachers to help him stay on top of every assignment. No, it will not make your child lazier. It will, in fact, over time renew his motivation to get back in the game.

A fabulous example of how to create small moments of success can be found in the teaching methods of master teacher Dorothy DeLay. She was the teacher of the brilliant Itzhak Perlman at the Juilliard School. Her complete method can be found in Carol Dweck's superb book, *Mindset*. You may ask, "How can the teaching methods of one of the greatest violin teachers apply to my struggling child?" The answer is simple, create small moments of success. One such example was when one of DeLay's students recalled a time when he was working on a difficult piece of music. DeLay listened patiently until he played a note particularly well. She then commented, "Now that's a beautiful sound."

Ms. DeLay explained how every note has to have a beautiful beginning, middle and end, leading into the next note. And the student thought, "Wow! If I can do it there, I can do it everywhere." It is worth repeating, *children, like any adult who suffers from low self-worth, often has difficulty in accepting positive feedback.* They are so used to hearing negative things about

Rule Five

themselves that when they do hear positive feedback, they dismiss it. In short, they don't take it in. Let me suggest a wonderful way to boost your child's receptivity. Before giving your child *or teenager a compliment, first alert him to what's coming:*

"Jackson, do you mind if I tell you something wonderful about yourself?" Asking for his permission will give him an extra few seconds to switch mindsets to prepare for some good news. When he says, *"Okay,"* say something like, *"I loved the way you helped mom in with the packages from her car. You were so calm and giving. Watching you do that made me feel that when I'm not around, I can count on you."*

Children and teenagers who continually underperform do not have a lack of will; they have a lack of success. Lots of well-meaning parenting experts talk about the value of learning the hard way, and while that's true for some kids, it is absolutely not true for others. Unlike some kids who can bounce back from defeat quickly, other kids get demoralized very, very quickly. Too often we tend to emphasize winners and losers. Well, there's also a third category: *those who have to be shown how to behave then they win.*

> If your 99% in, you're 100% out!

One quick word of caution: Be brief and calm, without a lot of fanfare. Too much fuss will create performance pressure. Keep it under 20 seconds. Unlike other communication principles, where sometimes we are inconsistent, expressing unrelenting optimism is the one rule we need to do 100% of the time. Kids, especially the more sensitive ones, tend to remember the one time we gave up on them. Think of it this way, if your 99% in, you're 100% out!

LIMIT PRAISE

In a misguided effort to gain a child's cooperation, some parents go overboard with phony praise, thinking it will make a child feel good about himself. It won't. Praise has two parts: what you tell your child, and even more importantly, what your child tells himself. If what you say doesn't match up with his or her own experience, you create all kinds of personal conflict, including avoidant behavior. Try to guard against unearned praise or over-praise.

Children who are told non-stop how brilliant, genius-like, or talented they are with no matching real-life experience run the risk of actually believing it, and that becomes a recipe for arrogance and obnoxiousness. Like cholesterol, there's a good kind of self-worth and a bad kind of self-worth. The good kind of self-worth communicates a relaxed humility, with no need to prove oneself to others. The bad kind elevates narcissistic self-love. It creates the obsessive adult-therapy addict who loves to hear and talk about himself. It breeds arrogance and superiority and repels friendships. Instead, our messages should be one of honest encouragement, not praise. Praise focuses on the end result. Encouragement focuses on the effort.

Telling a child, "Good job!" or how proud you are is not nearly as powerful as describing their effort: *"Michelle, you really stayed focused on that math test and you got the result you wanted." "You worked hard for it and it paid off."* Where's the praise? None! Just descriptive recognition of effort, which, in turn, makes the child think about their skills and how they applied them. Encouragement is a much stronger incentive than praise: praise focuses on the end result, but encouragement focuses entirely on the effort.

> Praise has two parts: what you tell your child, and even more importantly, what your child tells himself

There is no better book to make the case against over-praise, prizes and bribes than Alfie Kohn's book, *Punished by Rewards*. Read it! It is an excellent book on this subject, and after you read it, you will probably not use bribes or other shallow methods to gain cooperation. Although they work in the short run, in the context of loving relationships bribes speak to our lowest common denominator of behavior.

RETURN TO PAST MOMENTS OF SUCCESS

Typically, when children experience a very upsetting moment or event, parents have a tendency to think, "Whew, I'm glad that's over." While that may be true, it is also wise to revisit that experience with your child at a later time. It can be an hour later, that night, a week, or anytime later. It shows respect for your child's capacity and sensitivity to remember their experiences.

"Rebecca, that was a big fight we had last week. I still feel bad about our yelling at each other. I really like the way we talked it through in the end."

We can leverage those moments by showing our children we can talk about anything and at any time. In order to work it out, we have to get it out. Haunting thoughts can make children feel guilty with no channel for relief. It can make them shut down and shut off. Returning to a past moment can also be applied to past triumphs as well.

One highly effective way to reinforce future successful behavior is to recall the details of past successes. The key is not to over-talk or overdo it. It's not a selling moment, it's a telling moment. For example, during a quiet moment you can say, "I *was just thinking about how respectful you were in the restaurant last night. You said hello to the waiter and you paid attention to your brother when he spoke to you. I could tell you liked yourself when you did those things."*

Consider a different example involving a third-grader who fell behind in his schoolwork and worked all weekend to catch up. Weeks later a wise parent reminds his child of that great "come-from-behind" effort. Recalling a behavior conveys to the child that his or her successes are so impressive that you continue to think about them well after they have occurred. Children often forget their successes. They live in the moment. It is a highly rewarding feeling to remember one's past achievements. Don't go overboard and pile on too much positive recalling though, as it could serve as a trigger for guilty and regressive behavior.

TRY STARTING CONVERSATIONS WITH, "I WAS JUST THINKING ABOUT…"

Children, like adults, find it satisfying when we remember to bring up shared experiences, even those that might be painful. I can't tell how many times I learn about parents who go out for dinner with their kids, had a lot of laughs playing basketball in the driveway, read a great story to their kids at night, had a silly fight over how to put a toy back together that broke, laughed in a fun way over something silly or ten million other experiences and never mention it the next day or any day. It is as though it never happened. Whatever those experiences are, try to bring some of them up the next day. It really shows your child how you carry them in your heart. It also helps your children learn how to express themselves in order for them to connect too.

"Sammy, I was just thinking about yesterday afternoon. It was so much fun with you on the driveway shooting hoops. It was hysterical the way we keep taking turns throwing the ball over our heads and trying to get it in the basket. I could have done it for hours with you. Boy were we laughing."

"Michelle, I was just thinking about the way you and I were trying on clothes in my closet last night. I loved doing that with you and seeing you in all those outfits. You really did look good in those bright colors. Let's do that again soon."

The 60-Second Test

Now that you're familiar with the *five parenting rules,* ask yourself, at what level of ease do you communicate each one? Notice which ones come to you more naturally and which ones need to be strengthened. In 30 days, track your excellent progress. *(circle each one).*

Rule One: Show A Complete Understanding

High level   Medium level   Low level

Rule Two: Talk With Respect

High level   Medium level   Low level

Rule Three: Promote A Family Culture of Truth

High level   Medium level   Low level

Rule Four: Enforce Consequences Consistently

High level   Medium level   Low level

Rule Five: Show Unrelenting Optimism

High level   Medium level   Low level

The Difficult Child

Cooperation is won through relationship, not power.
—MARK L. BRENNER

One father with two very different teenage sons was telling me, "One kid I'm putting through college, the other I wanna put through a wall." Parents often wonder, "Was my child born this way?" The answer is probably yes. Some children can calm down within a few minutes of conflict; others take a lot longer. Difficult children are almost always late bloomers. Some have biological issues, some are related to natural delays, and others are related to emotional histories. Difficult children do not have to lead to difficult relationships.

> Difficult children do not have to lead to difficult relationships

Being realistic about how long something will take, always increases tolerance and patience. Nothing changes in five minutes. It makes no difference if we want to lose weight, get in shape or break a bad habit. Think about the last time you made a big psychological change. How long did it take you? Bottomline: Don't keep looking for light-bulb moments, especially if you are in the "repair" phase of your relationship. Resist getting drawn into magical thinking where you come to believe, the worst is over, or "my child's behavior will change by tomorrow." It won't. Yet, there is good news! Difficult children don't stay difficult.

The single biggest clue with a difficult child is their own

Rules without relationship lead to rebellion

natural temperament. Many researchers have studied temperament, including the classic research works of psychiatrists Thomas and Chess, and have concluded children fall into three main temperament categories: easy, difficult, and slow-to-warm-up. If we do not know the counter-intuitive ways to tamp down their inner psychological and/or physical battles, we wind up ratcheting up their tension and anxiety. As a result, these children will give us a predictable stress response. *You never win cooperation on the strength of your power or arguments, you win cooperation on the strength of your relationship.*

Two parenting rules that must never be violated with difficult children are *Speaking with Respect* and *Showing Unrelenting Optimism*. If this is your relationship, I strongly suggest that you temporarily put aside all consequences for about two weeks. It is worth repeating: Rules without relationship lead to rebellion. Instead, pour all your energy into applying the other four parenting rules. Really get them down so they become natural to say and do. After all, what's a few more weeks of letting certain behaviors slide while you re-establish emotional trust.

PLACE ON BAN ON YOUR ANGER

During the relationship reset, you must keep your temper in check. Temporarily place a ban on showing your anger and frustration. Unlike showing natural anger from time to time (controlled, of course) with a typical child, a struggling or oppositional child must RARELY see you lose your cool and explode. An angry tone gets translated as, "I knew you didn't believe in me!"

Within the first two-weeks of your new reset, your child will do everything — and I mean everything — to make you return to your old ways. Stay cool under fire. You've come too far to turn back now. If when preparing lunch you hear: *"you*

The Difficult Child

made the sandwich wrong, you always make it wrong." Just say, *"That's true, show me again how to make it right."* Don't show them who's the boss, show them who's in control. Never match your child's intensity, especially if your child is already high-strung and wound tight. Give no emotional energy to unwanted behavior. If your child amps up, you amp down! Do not energize negativity with extra words. Maintain super high levels of respect *(Rule Three)*, especially during moments of conflict. Remember, the emotional trust you build each day with your children or teenagers is only for that day. When you stop, your good work will stop and your relationship will experience another setback. If we slip too many times, it can take many more months to win back emotional trust again. Your own self-control will become the tipping point for your child or teenager to make their transformation.

This cute classic story of "The Patient Grandfather" makes this point perfectly.

> *A grandfather and his badly behaved three-year-old grandson have garnered all the attention at a supermarket. Granddad is working his way around, saying in a quiet and controlled voice, "Easy, William, we won't be long. Easy, boy." Another outburst, and the check-out girl hears Granddad again calmly saying: "It's okay, William, just a couple more minutes and we'll be out of here. Hang in there, boy." At this point the little boy is throwing items out of the cart, and the grandfather says again in a calm quiet voice, "William, William, relax buddy, don't get upset. We'll be home in five minutes; stay cool, William." Very impressed, the woman who checked out his groceries closes the line and rushes outside, where the grandfather is loading his groceries and the boy into the car. She says to the grandfather, "It's none of my business, but you were amazing in there. I don't know how you did it. That whole time, you*

kept your composure, so elegant, and no matter how loud and disruptive he got, you just calmly kept saying things would be okay. William is very lucky to have you as his grandfather." "Thank you," says the grandfather, "but you see I'm William, and that little son-of-a-bitch over there is Kevin!"

LATE BLOOMERS

The parenting landscape today is nothing like it used to be. Bringing some children through full development today is really a 21-year process, sometimes even longer. People say it never used to be that way. At the same time, as in all previous generations, there have always been late bloomers. Just Google great historical men and women and you'll be amazed to learn who lived at home longer than you thought. The point is, every family has at least one member who is a late bloomer and when we underestimate certain developmental issues, we can unwittingly do long term damage. Before we adopt this one-size-fits-all approach to teach children "life lessons learned the hard way," we need to know how to teach those life lessons "the right way," especially with children who are late bloomers. As educator Fred O. Gosman used to say, "Children allowed to develop at their own speed will usually win the race of life."

Many parenting experts who are invited to speak at schools have a simple message; "Stop all the spoiling and feeling messages" and just tell your kids, "Do what I tell you." These experts often point to themselves or those in their audiences as examples of growing up with little guidance and even less attention." "Our parents barely knew what grade we were in, let alone helped us with homework." The speaker then says, "Look at us. We turned out okay!" But, did

> Children allowed to develop at their own speed will usually win the race of life

we? What these speakers never ask is for a show of hands of how many in the audience (or their own brothers or sisters), who didn't turn out okay. The truth is, too many in those audiences are still silently struggling with high conflict marriages, anxiety, depression, addictions, divorce, and/or strained relationships with their own children.

The wisdom of knowing how and when to teach those life lessons makes all difference in the world. Of course, for some children, sometimes the hard way is the right way. The great comedian Buddy Hackett used to say, "I was raised in a family with only two choices on the menu: take it or leave it."

Gratuitous and silly spoiling for every want is very different from giving your children the extra support they need in school or at home. You can't speed up the natural development of a late bloomer. We all know that in life it's not how you start, it's how you finish. Parents need to give themselves permission to keep the scaffolding up around a late bloomer for as long as it takes. Whether it's helping them with their homework, staying organized, reading chapters when they're too tired, helping them finish a school project or lying down with them at night to help them get to sleep. It's cheeky to say, "Don't be a helicopter parent" (a phrase first used as early as 1969), but it's not always as simple as letting your child go it alone and *presto*, "lesson learned." Only you know your child's struggles and the right ways to help. Don't let other people get into your head and make you feel guilty.

DOING VS. EMOTIONAL DEVELOPING

> *There's a cute joke about a couple who sent out their very first birth announcement: "We are pleased to announce the birth of our son, Dr. Jacob Cohen." As parents we can all see a little of our own expectations for our children's future in that funny announcement. In our excitement to help our children achieve more,*

we must remember that although the desire to achieve is a natural life force, a future realized too soon holds tremendous risks.

Too often we read a headline about someone's brilliant life gone terribly wrong. In the blink of an eye what can start out as a natural talent can become an unhealthy obsession when we neglect emotional readiness. Even the most decorated Olympic champion in the history of the Olympic Games, Michael Phelps (with 28 medals, 25 of them gold) revealed his desire to end his life due in part to self-worth issues. He told ESPN that in 2014 he struggled to "figure out who he was outside the pool." In his own words, "I was a train wreck. I was like a time bomb waiting to go off. I had no self-esteem, no self-worth. I felt lost." Imagine this from the greatest swimmer of all time! Such raw honesty is a precious gift to all of us to elevate emotional maturity and relationship skills above everything else, including talent.

How many adults do we all know who have achieved tremendous success in their professional lives, but, sadly, remain destructive to themselves as well as with their spouses, children, extended family members and friends in their private lives?

In the context of raising children, the number one question to ask is not, *"How much is my child doing?"* but rather, *"How well is my child developing emotionally?"* It's easy for parents to get caught up in telling each other all the great things their children are doing.

"Did I tell you Ben is in the new leadership program?"
"Annie is already preparing for her SAT's."
"Stevie has the lead in the school play."
"Lilly is the head counselor at her summer camp."

We all want to feel that kind of pride. Who wouldn't? At the same time, telling others about our children's accomplishments may only be half the story. The other half rarely gets told. It may be hard to imagine saying:

"Michael is the editor of his newspaper, but he's having trouble making friends and fitting in."

The Difficult Child

"My Emily already knows what she wants to be, but she struggles with anxiety, perfectionism and eating issues."

No child or teenager should have to live in silence while suffering through feelings of isolation, mood swings, depression or intemperate anxiety just so parents can maintain bragging rights. Children must know at an early age that we value their emotional development and our relationship with them above everything else! When parents emphasize family relationships and emotional readiness first, achievement will follow in more natural ways. If we miss that emphasis, we increase the risks of our children falling behind, or worse, years later, falling apart. Sometimes we need to delay, modify or even withdraw a child from a program or a school, (no matter how great it's reputation) because the fit may no longer be a fit. It takes enormous courage and faith to act on that decision.

When you elevate emotional development over physical achievements, I have no doubt that one day in the very near future you will receive a call from your son or daughter saying, *"Mom, where have you been? I've been texting and calling you all day with no answer. I was worried about you. I was calling because I just miss you!"* Inside you will smile warmly and think, *"How great is this feeling!"*

A study at the Stanford University School of Business tracked a group of MBAs ten years after they graduated. The result? Grade-point average had no bearing on their success, but, what did was their ability to communicate ideas and motivate others. Academic and other performance skills-based testing is not the only metric. We should also equally value creativity, integrity, motivation and, of course, emotional intelligence.

Scoring higher grades in the classroom, achieving more status on the playing field or getting into a better college for the wrong reasons, must never be elevated above balanced development. Never!

Parents whose children show early signs of emotional stress typically think it's just a phase, especially with high-achieving children who struggle with perfectionism. If we don't attend to those early behavior issues properly, years later as we're putting together a list of potential colleges for our kids to attend, we may also find ourselves putting together a list of potential therapists. As a clinician, I'm certainly not suggesting that taking a child to see a therapist means that the parent-child relationship is the cause. Not at all. We are all born with challenges and sometimes the help of a talented therapist can make all the difference in the world, and we shouldn't hesitate to find the right one. The point I want to emphasize is that if our 'parenting style' becomes a part of the problem, it is not likely our children will accept our help.

HOW TO GIVE POSITIVE FEEDBACK WITH A DIFFICULT CHILD

Children, (like any adult) who suffer from low self-worth, often has difficulty in accepting positive feedback. They are so used to hearing negative things about themselves that when they do hear positive feedback, they dismiss it. In short, they don't take it in. Let me suggest a wonderful way to boost your child's receptivity. Before giving your child or teenager a compliment, first alert him to what's coming: *"Andrew, do you mind if I tell you something fantastic that I saw you do earlier?"*

Asking for his permission first will give him an extra few seconds to switch mindsets to prepare for the good news. Be sure you wait a few beats for his answer. When he says, *"Okay,"* say something like, *"I loved the way you walked into your brother's room this morning. Your face was so calm and relaxed. Your body was calm too. Did you feel it?"* One quick word of caution: Be brief without a lot of animation. Too much fuss will create performance pressure. Keep it under 20 seconds.

> Children, (like any adult) who suffer from low self-worth, often has difficulty in accepting positive feedback.

THE DIFFICULT TEENAGER

If you are in the repair phase with your teenager, begin by having a sit-down with your teenager and announce a fresh start, much like we did when we introduced the *house rules (page 103)*. It should be a serious but brief conversation, no more than 10 minutes. *Let your son or daughter feel your positive energy, optimism, calm and new self-awareness.* Maintain relaxed eye contact.

"Alex, there's been too much tension and too much distance between us. I have lost touch with the right way to talk and the right way to show you respect. I'm going to make BIG changes. Really BIG, and I take full responsibility for what has happened between us. All this conflict has been my fault. I am determined to return to earlier times of happiness and laughter. I want you to watch the new way I control my moods, my temper and my patience. Here's the best part: I can't wait to start!"

Here are some more teenager relationship tips.

1. Spend one on one time...

Next, take your teenager out for breakfast, for tea, or do a Sunday walk. Make it a habit every week. Even if they resist, you insist. It tells your child, "You are worth spending time with."

2. Develop a sense of humor...

The fastest way to reduce distance between two people is a good laugh. Lighten up! Don't take yourself so seriously. Try telling your kids a funny story and ask that they tell one too. Even if it's corny, everyone laughs!

3. Have fun together....

Go bowling, miniature golf, camping. In other words, do something unexpected together and laugh.

4. *Talk about things that don't matter...*

If all you ever talk about are problems, you have a problem relationship. Start talking about little things that aren't life changing! Learn to sometimes talk abut things that don't matter.

"You know Kenny, I've always wondered if you open a manhole cover on the street, how deep do they go down? What do you think?"

5. *Write notes*:

Let your children find personal notes from you in back packs and pockets. This is a marvelous way to reinforce that they are a priority and live in your heart. *"Blake, I'm making your favorite tonight for dinner. Can't wait to see you. Love, Mom."*

DOUBLE DOWN ON EXPRESSING OPTIMISM (RULE FIVE)

"Michael, no matter what, I will never stop believing in your ability to control yourself." Changing a child's negative self-image is a process of thousands of positive small comments that fall way under the radar of most parent-child interactions: Regardless of the difficulty your child is experiencing, do not use 'special language,' use normalizing language.

"Michelle, *"I noticed that you came down the stairs so quietly."*

"Norman, I noticed when you started your math homework, you knew just where to find your book."

"Thanks for closing the car door quietly."

Most parents feel uneasy and even silly in recognizing such small obvious behaviors. Still, by concentrating on those actions, the positive changes you see in your child's attitude will be dramatic.

Typically, non-compliant or stubborn children who have been constantly corrected and criticized at home and school do not initially respond well when recognized for smaller efforts. Be prepared for strong negative reactions.

It's an odd experience to tell your child something positive about himself and have him take it in the wrong way. One mother recently asked me why each time she gave her 11-year-old son praise about being a "good brother," he would act out aggressively. After investigating a bit more, it became clear that her son held tremendous resentment for his younger brother. The reason he was acting out was because when his mother would praise him for being "a good brother," he was secretly wishing for bad things to happen to his brother. His guilt became his trigger for aggression. That is one reason praise can sometimes backfire, it must match our internal experiences.

As we discussed earlier, one way to help your child accept positive feedback is to first ask for his permission. *"Robert, would you mind if I tell you something wonderful about you that I've noticed?"* Then wait for his answer. This allows him an opportunity to switch mindsets, so he can prepare for the good news. By the way, this also works well with adults who also have low self-worth issues. I also suggest using the words *successful* and *successfully* to describe your child's progress. *"Danny, you were successful in how you controlled your mood with your sister just now."* Do not be swayed when he says, "Why do you keep using that word? Stop it! I'm tired of hearing it!" Tell him, *"This is how I see you, and that word describes you perfectly."*

Many parents are under the false impression that expressing too much appreciation somehow makes a defiant child feel more empowered. Appreciation will not empower a child — it will calm him. *"Thank you, David for accepting my 'no' answer without arguing with me." "Katie, I appreciate how you brought me the vacuum cleaner right away."* Your increased belief and confidence will be the biggest contributor to his new-found success.

As your child's self-image is shifted from failure to success as a result of your unrelenting optimism, a new sense of self will begin to emerge. *"I know you will do the right thing next time."* To be more convincing, adjust your tone of voice by putting more calm and heart into your words: *"David, I know when I leave the room, you will turn the computer off in five minutes."* It's more of a quiet "telling" than "selling."

WHEN YOU GIVE A CONSEQUENCE, DON'T PILE ON MORE

When your difficult child blows past a limit and refuses to complete a consequence, resist piling on more consequences. Difficult and defiant children typically like to prove how they can take whatever punishment you throw at them.

Do not set up a contest of wills by adding more consequences. They will dig in and prove they can take whatever you dish out. The problem with piling on more demands is that it creates feelings of hopelessness. We see this pattern in adults when they pile up too much debt, or gain too much weight. It can makes you feel: "What's the use? There's no way out!"

> Difficult and defiant children typically like to prove how they can take whatever punishment you throw at them

One way to help a child overcome defiant behavior is by providing a consequence that he can successfully complete. Instead of giving a difficult child an impossible consequence, keep it manageable. *"Darren, I see the dirty look you are giving me. You know the rule in our house: no disrespect. I know deep down you feel bad. Take a 'time break' for 3 minutes."*

Most parents do the opposite and threaten more punishment with even stronger consequences. Be sure to show your quiet and grateful appreciation after he completes it. *"David, I know you resisted cleaning your room in the beginning. Still, I had no doubt you would do it. Thank you so much."* Do not forget to use the Broken Record. *(page 96)*

IN OUR FAMILY

A great expression to use when children compare what you allow to their friends' family is, *'in our family.'* "Dad, in Ben's house his parents allow video games before bed." Then you can reply,

"Danny, I have no doubt that's true. In our family, you know we don't. We have different rules and I know you respect them."

The words *"in our family"* should become a themed expression for years to come. It reinforces the parents' value system (in contrast with other families), and gives the child a feeling of identity. Use it frequently including when you see other kids (or adults) acting inappropriately in public too. *"Wow, Danny look at that boy two booths down. We would never wear audio headsets at the dinner table. Look at all the family members sitting together, they don't even look at each other. Our family would never do that. We like talking and looking at each other."*

BACK TALK

Too many parents stand in fear of their child's rejection. One part of a parent's rationalization to accept a child's backtalk is the false thinking that it will teach the child how to stand up for himself. We all want our children to have confidence. It is a quality, combined with humility, that can take us far in life. However, the wrong kind of confidence breeds arrogance and a know-it-all attitude. Backtalk from children leads to bully behavior and obnoxiousness. When your child launches into back talk, give a counter-intuitive response.

"Brian, I know it bothers you when you try to put me down. Why don't you start again, and tell me what you want me to know, this time with respect." If your child continues in a tone of disrespect, tell him, *"Because you have decided to continue talking in a sarcastic tone, our conversation is over now. I have too much respect for you and me to allow such talk. You have tremendous anger towards me. When you're*

ready to talk with a caring tone, I want to start again. I'll be in the den. I look forward to starting again."

FOUL LANGUAGE

If your younger child shows a sudden increase in foul language, he is either experimenting, under someone's influence, or carrying inside his fair share of anger. One suggestion to help him get his foul mouth under control is to recommend alternative expressions. At the very least, suggest less-offensive alternatives, such as "crap," or "crud." Let him make up his own animated epithets. The idea of you allowing your child sometimes to express himself graphically will surprise him in a positive way. Still hold to your family standards and again invoke the phrase, "in our family."

Having said all this, if you believe your child is not deliberately trying to be disrespectful, but is using filthy language to emphasize something give him a second chance to get it right. *"Jacob, wait. Start over! I know you realize you are talking in a disgusting way."* When he self-corrects, quietly say, "I knew you would figure it out and say it elegantly. I agree completely."

At the same time, if your teenager uses a foul word that truly fits the situation, and again is not saying it in a gratuitous or disrespectful way, let it go and reflect back his seriousness. Henry, there's no doubt that you want nothing to do with your friend Ted at school after what he did to you. He was a shit head.

One final note, if you hear one of your younger child's friends use filthy language around your child, or other children (for example in a carpool), you should lay out a specific, matter-of-fact family rule about cursing: *"Alex, in our family, those words are not allowed. If you say it again, I'll have to take you home right now to your parents."* Don't be shy about enforcing bad language rules with your children's friends. A simple, *"We don't allow that language in our family,"* delivered in a serious, I-mean-business tone, will startle many of his friends into silence and reinforce in your own child your seriousness.

WHINING AND COMPLAINING

When dealing with a meltdown, do not set a time limit on how long you allow your child to whine or complain. *"Justin, quit crying already! Act like a big boy! I'm going to ignore you if you keep complaining!"*

Obviously, it's incredibly obnoxious to listen to non-stop whining and carrying on. The secret is to ignore his obnoxious behaviors without ignoring the child, all the while maintaining a very high level of respect.

"Justin, you can take as long as you want to remain upset. I know this is not easy for you to accept. I also know you understand why I am not going along with what you want." When your child sees he does not get under your skin, and really comes to believe you will not return to your old ways, he will likely begin to cooperate. You have to be willing to go through this test period.

The Difficult Spouse

*Deep inside us, we know what every family therapist knows;
the problems between parents, become the problems within the children.*
—ROGER GOULD, PSYCHIATRIST

This is a difficult chapter to write. Author Franklin P. Jones was famous for saying, "The most difficult year of marriage is the one you're in." Spouses who are in "high-conflict marriages" suffer every day. In the beginning, each blames the other, thinking it's just stereotypical male or female patterned behavior. The great comedians on stage make us laugh hysterically from some of these truths. Unfortunately, as the years pass, a darker truth emerges and more serious mental health issues may come to light.

Trying to love someone who is in denial about his or her psychological problems is far more exhausting than loving someone with a physical illness. When a spouse cares for another with a physical illness, he or she usually receives back tremendous feelings of appreciation. Contrast that with spouses who are in denial about their emotional problems. The only thing caring spouses receive back is more abuse. Outsiders do not see the emotional trauma because there are no physical marks or bruises. It's all on the inside.

Spouses and family members have learned how to put on a good show in front of others, including in their

> The most difficult year of marriage is the one you're in

communities. Emotional traumas are easily hidden by those who have learned the art of emotional masquerade. I have seen many spouses sink into depression, addiction, change their personalities or become emotionally numb as a result of being married to an unaware spouse who lives to blame and hurt. Troubled spouses are always trying to make you feel, "There's nothing wrong with me. It's you! You need the meds!"

In one instance, a wife was fighting with her husband about how uncaring and disinterested he seemed to be about how her day went. During the fight the husband asked,

"Honey, don't you want to know why?" She responded in her usual way, *"No, I just want you to care."*

Her lack of interest in discovering why he felt uninterested is the very reason he has lost interest. Her refusal to examine her own behaviors includes why her children also withdraw from her. It's exhausting being in relationship with someone who's defensive. Everything requires an explanation, even a simple text message becomes a back and forth argument. You quickly learn not to correct or engage in order to avoid conflict.

In general, having a serious mental disorder means having a rigid and unhealthy pattern of thinking and behaving, no matter what the situation. Toxic people lack empathy, compassion, kindness and respect. All difficult spouses have one trait in common: They never ask, *"What am I missing? What have I done to cause such upset?"* They constantly blame others and remain oblivious to their own behaviors. In their own mind they see the world correctly. They may have kind hearts on the inside, but on the outside they lack consistent self-awareness and emotional warmth. One of their signature ways of behaving is when they hurt you, they act as though you hurt them. One patient told me, "My husband makes me sick and then takes me to the best doctors."

This can become even more complicated if they have extended

> Toxic people lack empathy, compassion, kindness and respect

family members who also share in defensive dysfunctional behaviors. If you are in such a marriage, resist being a part of the conspiracy created by all of them who attempt to rewrite reality. As Dr. Tian Dayton writes in her extraordinary psychodrama book, *The Living Stage*.

"Reality gets rewritten as family members attempt to bend it toward making it less threatening and more in line with their sense of 'normal.' This bending of reality is part of the 'crazy making' world of the addicted/traumatizing family in which family members lose their grasp on what constitutes normal functioning. Family members often collude in this denial, and anyone who attempts to turn the spotlight onto the harsh reality of dysfunction may be perceived as disloyal. They risk being cut off if they get too close to the underlying despair that the family does not want to look at. The family may 'kill the messenger' by making them the problem, a phenomenon known as 'scapegoating.' The risk becomes even greater when we pass down the 'denial trait' to our children. 'Your uncle loves you, he just has a lot on his mind!' Unwittingly, young children and teenagers are brought into this conspiracy as they are taught that rapid shifts in mood, inappropriate smiling, flat affect and a general denial of emotional truths are all accepted as normal." You must protect your children from this false reality by vigilantly applying A Family Culture of truth *(Rule Three)*.

The decision to remain in a marriage with a spouse who has serious emotional problems is deeply complicated and individual in nature. The decision and consequences of staying or leaving are gut-wrenching. It can sometimes feel like there are no good options. But there are options.

FINDING PROFESSIONAL HELP

When asked who started their brawl during the 1981 National Hockey League's Stanley Cup playoffs, New York Ranger, Barry Beck, famously said: "We have only one person to blame, and that's the other." I have never seen a high-conflict marriage where each spouse contributes equally to the dysfunction. Never! On the contrary, it is always one spouse who, from the beginning, has been at the heart of the problem.

If you suffer in such a marriage, I strongly suggest letting your spouse know (always with a caring tone), that your marriage cannot survive without outside help. Find a professional who is trained to identify these behavior patterns quickly (sometimes within the first session and often within five). Good therapists promote a culture of truth, bad therapists negotiate peace plans. Stay away from therapists who advocate emotional equivalency. In other words, "You are both somewhat equally at fault" and "you just need to do more" of that phony active listening. Destructive patterns of relating to one another need to be revealed in a safe, but honest way during these counseling sessions. If you find yourself with a simplistic and superficial therapist, don't even finish the session. Leave! A well-intentioned but misguided therapist can do real damage, especially if you are barely holding on to your sanity.

I also recommend that the therapist be a family systems therapist who works with the whole family. These therapists are trained in such a way to understand that no individual member of a family can be truly understood in isolation, but rather as a part of the entire family constellation. *That means seeing each family member individually and together including your children.* The field of family systems therapy is replete with validating research that a family systems approach is considerably more effective and faster, especially with high conflict marriages. Family therapists have mastered all the boundary issues and know how to create an atmosphere where all members trust the therapist. Unfortunately, most therapists are not well-trained in this area or, if at all.

Other advantages of using the same therapist, is that you will be better at evaluating the quality of the therapist's work since you will be able to see first hand if your spouse is manipulating the process. If you go to separate therapists, it is much too easy for you to become lost in the process.

For younger children, it is essential that the therapist also be well-versed in play therapy. They will have a separate and fully stocked playroom for play sessions. Be very wary of therapists who have only one office with some scattered toys or board games to give the appearance they work with young children. You can't work properly with young children when they see a serious business desk, office chairs, sophisticated paintings, sculptures and a library of books all intended for adults. The room should speak for itself with an array of appropriate toys. An experienced play therapist will know how to decode their play and arrive more quickly on what the child needs. What words are for adults, the right toys become for children.

There is help out there. Now that you have a better idea of what you may need, begin by doing a thoughtful Internet search on what issues you are seeing in your family. Also, ask your closest friends, outside family members and your clergy.

TELLING YOUR CHILDREN THE TRUTH ABOUT A SPOUSE

Never shrink from telling your children the truth about a spouse, family member or anyone else who suffers from a psychological disorder. It should be discussed with the highest degree of caring and respect. This kind of dialogue should continue throughout their full development and well beyond. One of my patients used to always tell me, "my parents used to hide things from me, like the truth."

Rarely do spouses change each other. They change as a result of their children pulling away from them emotionally. I have seen these transformations happen countless times. When kids speak up spontaneously from their hearts why they don't want to spend time with a parent,

> **Rarely do spouses change each other. They change as a result of their children pulling away from them emotionally**

that parent really takes it in. *"Honey, now I see how I have been making you feel. I am so so sorry. I am stopping."*

Finally, as each child becomes older and more comfortable in hearing and speaking the truth about their own family members, they will feel more at ease with themselves, as well. They will also become better at spotting odd behaviors in others outside their family.

THE EFFECT ON CHILDREN

One of the most common questions parents ask is, what is the effect on children whose parents live in a high conflict marriage, are divorced or parent with opposite communication styles and values? They are relieved to learn that it will *not* be the marriage, but the individual parent-child relationship that will have the greater influence on a child's mental health and future happiness. Obviously, having both parents share the same parenting values is best; however, the earliest awareness of relationships by young children is not experienced through the eyes of their parents' compatibility, but through their own feelings of emotional compatibility with each parent. You can feel great relief in knowing that your children can still wind up emotionally healthy and balanced, as long as they have one parent whom they share an extraordinary relationship with.

Parents who are the most unhappy in their marriages, need to be acutely aware that they do not look to their children to fill the lost affection and respect that they once had with their spouse. Those unmet needs can manifest in over-spoiling their children in order to be perceived as 'the good parent.' Such marriages can become even more complicated when feelings of aloneness trigger painful memories from their own childhood where their emotional needs were also not met. Those combined painful memories lead parents to keep giving in and giving more, in the hope they get more affection and attention from their children. *The takeaway:* Pay more attention to what your children need developmentally and not just to what they want in the moment.

STRATEGIES TO MOTIVATE YOUR SPOUSE TO GET HELP

One strategy is to recruit outside family members or friends to give spontaneous feedback to your spouse. This strategy will initially cause more conflict, but it has the potential to positively influence your spouse to get outside help. The key is having those friends or outside family members talk openly about how these destructive behaviors have affected them. With this strategy those who speak up risk losing their relationship with that person. Still, it is a risk worth taking.

A second strategy that is even more powerful involves telling your spouse if they do not get help you will separate. This must not be a bluff. The risk is worth it because you flex your courage and strength, showing you no longer will take the abuse. Telling your spouse he or she needs to leave the house is a call to action *not* heard before. Typically, especially for men, the risk of losing their marriage and family will often produce quicker cooperation. Men typically respond well when there is an emergency, or a real threat.

You must however, follow through. Before you green light this strategy, make sure you are working with a seasoned licensed therapist, who has expertise with trial separations. There are many rules of conduct that must be followed exactly, including no dating, no spending money on big purchases (cars, jewelry etc.), no impulsive dropping in, etc. It is a cooling off period, not a license to date. The rules you put in place (your therapist will tell you all of them), must be maintained vigilantly. It usually takes between three to nine months to know if a trial separation will work.

A third strategy promises the highest likelihood of success. Assuming you have brought your children up with *A Family Culture of Truth* (Rule Three), let your children have a role in being the messenger. *"Mom/ Dad, please, get help. I am hurting the way you treat me."* To participate in this process, children should be at least 12-years-old. I suggest doing some rehearsals with your children. *"Please, Daddy, please get help. Your moods scare me."* Or, *"Mommy, you make me feel bad about myself. I never know what mood you will be in."* You will also need to prepare them for the likely guilt feelings they will have for taking sides and being accused of being part of a conspiracy against that parent. In the long run they will feel the grit of their own courage and power and come to know it was not their fault.

In time your children will likely be the ones convincing your spouse to get help. Nothing will incentivize a father or mother faster than hearing from one or all of their children about how hard it is to be with them.

HOW TO REMAIN EMOTIONALLY HEALTHY

By now you know better than anyone there is no winning! American novelist Anne Lamott tells us: There are three things you can't change: the past, the truth and the other person. With that in mind, when you're finding yourself becoming more angry, more depressed and less patient, it is probably because you are trying to change one of those three things.

If you are married to a spouse who has a serious mental issue, your first step is to fight against the tendency to remain in denial. Educate yourself in every way possible on what condition they have, and how to cope.

1. *Don't be a martyr.* Some spouses who live with someone who is emotionally disturbed typically have learned not to express their own feelings to the rest of the family. They promote a martyr profile where keeping the peace becomes their singular mission. They sweep most of their own feelings under the rug for fear of losing approval or affection from others. As an unintended consequence, they prevent other family members from expressing themselves too. Everyone learns to stay quiet and suck it up. As a result, everyone suffers in silence as it creates an

atmosphere of superficiality. Sadly, a martyr style profile is a faulty carry-over from childhood and it must be repaired. Solution: *Be real.*

2. *Let go of that which you cannot control.* Visualize handing those issues over to a Higher Power and sincerely believe it. It really works.

3. *Make self-care a priority.* Although you may not have a lot of time, be sure you are eating right, exercising and socializing. If you can't prepare a good meal, keep healthy snack bars and fruit nearby. Do your best to take a twenty-minute power nap every day and fully pamper yourself at least once a week.

4. At the very least, *take a 15-minute daily brisk walk* to release some physical tension. Your biggest and best ideas can also come from this. Practice mindfulness techniques such as deep breathing and meditation. Protect your own individuality through hobbies, self-care and friendships.

5. *Spend less time – or no time – with toxic people.* As they say, "Stay away from negative people, they have a problem for every solution." These are individuals who do not know how to show empathy. They may mean well, but don't behave well. If you are not sure if someone is toxic, here's a clue: After being with him or her, if you feel drained and depleted, the person is toxic. In other words, they make you feel worse.

6. *Pour yourself into your children.* Pour yourself into your children's development and your relationship with them. This joy will be tremendously satisfying. However, avoid excessively spoiling your children as a result of feeling emotional emptiness from your marriage and/or the fear of being rejected. Know the difference between spoiling and supporting.

7. *Remain optimistic.* Wake up every morning and make a conscious effort to reflect a positive attitude. As leading psychiatrist Dr. David Burns likes to say: "If you change your thinking, you'll change your mood." By maintaining

this new mindset, you are preparing for the greatest life surprise of all: the unexpected! If you change from "it will never happen," to "let's see what happens," you are leaving room for possibility and change. You will discover that you have more energy and better moods. This new mindset is deceptively simple, but it works. Author and life coach Lisa Hayes frames it this way: "Be careful what you say about yourself; you're listening!"

8. *Practice the pause.* When *angry,* pause. When in *doubt,* pause. When *tired,* pause.

A FEW PROFILES OF PSYCHOLOGICAL DISORDERS

NARCISSISTIC PERSONALITY DISORDER

Narcissistic behavior can be more easily understood if you think of it as a combination of two things: *excessive* self-infatuation and a lack of expressing empathy towards others at the right time and in the right way. People with this disorder believe they are of primary importance in everybody's life or to anyone they meet. It is also known as the "it's all about me" syndrome. The old joke about a man on his first date who keeps talking about himself and then pauses to say, "Enough about me. What do you think of me?"

Those with narcissistic personality disorder often display snobbish and patronizing attitudes to those they feel are below them. Frequently, others, including family members, will become subjected to their bursts of anger and moodiness when you don't go along with what they want. Everything related to a relationship problem is always the other's fault. When they're not combative, narcissists can be exceedingly charming and fun to be with. They often use gifts as ways to keep family members and friends indebted and loyal. They are highly manipulative and completely blind to the true emotional needs of others and how to satisfy those needs. If you know someone dating a narcissist, tell them... run! Even with a well-trained therapist, the narcissist always attempts to establish superiority and engage in manipulation and mind games in order to sabotage their own therapy process.

An individual with this disorder will do better in group therapy than individual therapy for one central reason: Individual therapy feeds his or her insatiable need for being at the center of everything, in effect having the therapist to themself! With a well run group therapy program, they will have much greater difficulty controlling the other members.

Narcissistic personality disorder is more prevalent in males than females, and is thought to occur in less than one percent of the general population. The APA (American Psychiatric Association) suggests that if an individual has at least five of these characteristics, he or she may have this disorder:

- *Has a grandiose sense of self-importance.* (e.g., exaggerates achievements and talents, expects to be recognized as superior without commensurate achievements)
- *Is preoccupied with fantasies of unlimited success, power, brilliance, beauty, or ideal love.*
- *Believes that he or she is "special" and unique* and can only be understood by, or should associate with, other special or high-status people (or institutions).
- *Requires excessive admiration. Has a very strong sense of entitlement. (e.g., unreasonable expectations of especially favorable treatment or automatic compliance with his or her expectations*
- *Is exploitative of others.* (e.g., takes advantage of others to achieve his or her own ends)
- *Lacks empathy.* (e.g., is unwilling to recognize the feelings and needs of others)
- *Is often envious of others* or believes that others are envious of him or her.

- *Regularly shows arrogant, haughty behaviors and know-it-all attitudes.*

BORDERLINE PERSONALITY DISORDER (BPD)

Borderlines are bullies whose bark is substantially bigger than their bite. They are abusive manipulators. Borderlines feel they are smarter than everyone else. If you yield when a borderline pushes, you've already lost the battle and things always get worse. Remember, your Borderline is like a child who tests your limits just to see how much he or she can get away with. Borderlines are emotionally underdeveloped and you must be willing to enforce boundaries. You absolutely *must* command respect — it's the only way to influence their behavior. With borderlines, when you stand up to them, they are likely to rebel or sulk. They might even get teary or weepy and accuse you of being insensitive or controlling. You may find yourself feeling guilty and apologizing for crimes you didn't commit. Passivity is the kiss of death in any relationship with a Borderline. Borderline personality disorder is mainly treated using psychotherapy, but medication may also be added.

Signs and symptoms may include: (*Mayo Clinic)

- *An intense fear of abandonment,* even going to extreme measures to avoid real or imagined separation or rejection.
- *A pattern of unstable intense relationships,* such as idealizing someone one moment and then suddenly believing the person doesn't care enough or is cruel.
- *Rapid changes in self-identity and self-image* that include shifting goals and values, and seeing yourself as bad or as if you don't exist at all.
- *Periods of stress-related paranoia and loss of contact with reality,* lasting from a few minutes to a few hours.

- *Impulsive and risky behavior*, such as gambling, reckless driving, unsafe sex, spending sprees, binge eating or drug abuse, or sabotaging success by suddenly quitting a good job or ending a positive relationship.
- *Suicidal threats or behavior or self-injury*, often in response to fear of separation or rejection.
- *Wide mood swings* lasting from a few hours to a few days, which can include intense happiness, irritability, shame or anxiety.
- *On-going feelings of emptiness.*
- *Inappropriate, intense anger*, such as frequently losing your temper, being sarcastic or bitter, or having physical fights.

BIPOLAR DISORDER

Bipolar disorder is a brain disorder that causes unusual shifts in mood, energy and activity level accompanied by abnormal behavior that disrupts life. Although there are technically five categories of Bipolar Disorder, the two most common are *Bipolar I and Bipolar II*. They are separate diagnoses. The main difference is a matter of severity.

People with *Bipolar I* disorder experience unusually intense emotional states that occur in distinct periods called "mood episodes." An overly-joyful or over-excited state is called a manic episode, and an extremely sad or hopeless state is called a depressive episode. Often, there is a pattern of cycling between mania and depression. This is where the term "manic depression" comes from. A person affected by Bipolar I disorder has had at least one manic episode in his or her life.

With *Bipolar II* disorder, one will experience severe depression and a less severe form of mania known as hypomania. Hypomania often masquerades as happiness and relentless optimism. Symptoms include flying suddenly from one idea to the next, having exaggerated self confidence, rapid and uninterruptible loud speech, increased energy, and a decreased need for sleep. Untreated, an episode of hypomania can last anywhere from a few days to several months. People experiencing hypomanic episodes are often quite pleasant to be around. They can often seem like the "life of the party" -- making jokes, showing a caring interest in other people or activities, and infecting others with their positive mood.

A severe form of this disorder is called Rapid-Cycling Bipolar Disorder. Rapid cycling occurs when a person has four or more episodes of major depression, mania, hypomania, or mixed states, all within a year. Rapid cycling seems to be more common in people who have their first bipolar episode at a younger age. Rapid cycling affects more women than men. People with an immediate family member who has bipolar are at higher risk. Still, biology is not destiny.

Persons diagnosed with Bipolar Disorder experience three times the rate of divorce as the general public. Currently, Bipolar Disorder cannot be identified through a blood test or a brain scan, but these tests can help rule out other factors that may contribute to mood problems, such as a stroke or thyroid condition. Bipolar Disorder can be treated successfully and can lead to a fully productive life. At the same time, Bipolar Disorder requires lifelong treatment, even during periods when the person is feeling better. Treatment is usually guided by a skilled psychiatrist (often through meds) and therapist, including group and or family counseling.

ALEXITHYMIA

Imagine biting into the most delicious summer fruits. A red juicy plum, a fresh yellow peach, a cold crisp Macintosh apple. Only one problem: You have a terrible cold and you have no taste. Your taste buds are flat. Alexithymics have flat affect and reactions tend to be detached when they talk.

Although they are generally good people with kind hearts, they lack significant emotional self-awareness. Generally speaking, Alexithymics do not know how to respond and satisfy other people's feelings. They struggle to find the right words because their emotional vocabulary is severely limited. It is super unsatisfying spending time with them.

The term was coined from the Greek a- (prefix meaning "lack"), lexis ("word") and thymos ("feelings"), and hence can be read literally as "a lack of words for feelings." They have trouble relating emotionally to others and tend to become uncomfortable during conversations. Typically they are incredibly stoic. They like to avoid emotional topics and focus more on concrete, objective statements.

Alexithymics are perceived by others as excessively logical, transactional and unsentimental. They are perplexed by other people's emotional reactions; give pedantic answers to practical questions; have a subdued response to art, literature or music; and have difficulty distinguishing between their emotional feelings and bodily feelings. They tend to be inflexible and react to relationship issues according to philosophy or principles rather than feelings.

GENERAL ANXIETY DISORDER (GAD)

Excessive symptoms of stress can include irritability and anger, anxiety, lack of motivation, fatigue, poor sleep, sadness or depression. Unfortunately, some forms of anxiety can take on a life of their own and interfere with normal functioning. Anxiety disorders are the single most common class of mental disorders affecting about 40 million adults.

Generalized Anxiety Disorder is a chronic irrational worry that can't be turned off. It shifts from one worry to another. Unlike panic disorder, which includes specific fears, those with Generalized Anxiety Disorder cannot articulate what they are worrying about. It's not uncommon for some adults with GAD to have medical disorders as well.

The anxiety and worry is associated with at least 3 of the following physical or cognitive symptoms (In children, only 1 symptom is necessary for a diagnosis of GAD.)

- *Edginess or restlessness.*
- *Tiring easily; more fatigued than usual.*
- *Impaired concentration or feeling as though the mind goes blank.*
- *Irritability (which may or may not be observable to others).*
- *Increased muscle aches or soreness.*
- *Difficulty sleeping (due to trouble falling asleep or staying asleep, restlessness at night, or unsatisfying sleep).*

I highly recommend reading Dr. David Burn's book 'When Panic Attacks.' This is a fabulous book that people say is a miracle cure.

DEPRESSION

Contrary to certain stereotypes about aging, depression is not a "normal" part of getting older. It is well known that when one spouse becomes depressed, the marriage becomes depressed. Depression erodes emotional and sexual intimacy, and substitutes it with pessimism, resentment and isolation. Even the most positive partner can be pulled into their spouses depression. Depressed couples are nine times more likely to divorce. With the right help, some forms of depression can be successfully treated. I highly recommend reading Dr. David Burn's book 'Feeling Good,' along with his other books on anxiety. When practiced properly, this can produce life-changing results.

The longer a non-depressed spouse lives with a depressed partner, the higher his or her own risk becomes for depression. An estimated 14 million adults suffer with depression. Depression isn't a little case of the blues. It's a physical illness as serious as diabetes or heart disease. A depressed spouse can't just "snap out of it" and become happy. When people are depressed, even minor decisions such as what to have for dinner can be overwhelming.

The Difficult Spouse

The deeper a depressed spouse sinks, the greater the risk for alcoholism, drug abuse, violence, and even suicide.

Although genetics often make us susceptible, any number of factors can trigger the slide, including prolonged or severe stress, financial problems, the birth of a child, a big loss or change in life, or for the seriously unprepared, parenthood. If you or your spouse experience at least five of the following symptoms, seek professional help immediately.

1. *Depressed mood most of the day, almost every day. Sadness, emptiness, or hopelessness.*
2. *Markedly diminished interest or pleasure in all or almost all activities nearly every day.*
3. *Significant weight loss or weight gain.*
4. *Inability to sleep or oversleeping nearly every day.*
5. *Psychomotor agitation or retardation nearly every day.*
6. *Fatigue or loss of energy nearly every day.*
7. *Feelings of worthlessness or excessive guilt (which may be delusional) nearly every day.*
8. *Diminished ability to think or concentrate, or indecisiveness, nearly every day.*
9. *Recurrent thoughts of death (not just fear of dying), recurrent suicidal ideation without a specific plan, or a suicide attempt, or a specific plan for committing suicide.*

Technology and Social Media

The most important factors in the life of their children are not the school, the television set, the playmates, or the neighborhood, but what the parents cherish, what they hate, and what they fear.

—THOMAS HORA

Every parenting book over the last 75 years makes reference to the new modern era and how difficult parenting has become. They all lay claim to how fast the world is changing. While true, today with download speeds matching electricity, an App for almost everything, addictive social media, self-driving cars, drone home delivery, AI avatars and space travel as the new frontier, we don't have a different world, we have a different universe! Ten to fifteen years from now, this is all going to feel like dial-up.

The Internet is clearly the television set of the 21st century. More than half of all children today use an online social network by the age of 10. And yes, it is addictive. It may not be included in today's DSM-5, but this technology and social media with swipes and clicks should be. Even the most relaxed

> The Internet is clearly the television set of the 21st century

parents recognize this high risk. A recent study has found that children between the ages of eight and 18 are either staring at an electronic screen, or using an electronic device a stunning eight hours a day. Some studies have it at even more! We check our phones about 80 times a day. Soon we will see warning alerts on our phones in the same way there are warning labels on the dangers of smoking cigarettes. Parents must get more serious in enforcing stricter limits with their children.

In her TED talk, "Connected, But Alone," Sherry Turtle says that our electronic devices reinforce the feeling that "No one is listening to me" and as a result, make us want to spend more time with social media. All these forces pull children (adults, too) into the labyrinth of aloneness. We may feel like we're connecting, but paradoxically we continue to increase social isolation. Of course, the digital age is here to stay and we need to stop lamenting its growth. At the same time we can do a better job of showing our kids how to live offline. They may get all their information from the Cloud, but we must not let them live in one.

Do 9-year-olds need to be texting each other where they want to meet up after school? We haven't even discussed the risks of cyber-bullying, pornography, depression, or the damaging physical side-effects of over-use, such as poor posture, eye strain, weight gain, and possibly even a rise in cholesterol levels. I can teach any average 11-year-old to drive a car, but if I put him in traffic, he'll crash, and we're putting our kids in too much traffic. Do kids really need to check their smart phones every fifteen-minutes to see how many "likes" they have, or to see new posted profile pages of kids they don't even know. While social media of course can be positive, unchecked it can also be like inhaling bus fumes.

In 2012, Christopher Carpenter of Western Illinois University published a study titled "Narcissism on Facebook" in the *Journal of Personality and Individual Differences.* Carpenter said that for the average narcissist, Facebook "offers a gateway for hundreds of shallow relationships and emotionally detached communication." It satisfies their needs for exaggerated sense of self-importance. In another recent study, titled "Sweden's Largest Facebook Study," results indicated that users who spend more time on Facebook tend to have lower self-worth. Other studies point to even more unintended consequences.

The JFK Medical Center finds that kids (and adults too) are developing mood, sleep and learning problems because their smart phones and digital tablets are keeping them awake at night. Too many of us are more connected to our devices than we are to each other.

EARLY CHILDHOOD

While you may be impressed that your five-year-old knows how to download an app, you shouldn't be! You are playing Russian roulette with your child's emotional development. Every week the Academy of Pediatrics changes it mind about what is good and not good when it comes to digital learning. *Never replace common sense with general online reading.*

Putting aside the obvious and wonderful benefits that new technologies offer children who have learning differences, more disturbing research is beginning to emerge regarding four, five and six-year-olds who are developing screen addictions. Medically speaking, continuous smartphone and tablet use stimulates the frontal cortex and increases dopamine levels, which in turn sends out the 'feel good' neuro-transmitters that play a key role in addiction. Even the vertical direction of swiping up and down till we come upon something we like, releases a dopamine fix. I strongly suggest taking the road less travelled and pulling way back on what you allow and won't allow your children to see and use. It's time to substitute real toys and put the electronics back where they belong—in the box. Even the late iconic visionary Steve Jobs knew to significantly limit his children from using his own inventions. We don't need more studies, we need more common sense. There are, of course, exceptions. Among those exceptions would be children with learning

> We don't need more studies, we need more common sense

differences, such as dyslexia or dyscalculia. Under these conditions, digital learning devices and software applications can make all the difference in the world.

A few years back at the International Consumer Electronics Show, a brand new toddler invention was unveiled: a portable potty trainer with an iPad holder. Let me give you a moment to think about that image. It was designed to keep your child occupied while learning to go to the bathroom on his own. Instead of downloading a poop, he's downloading an App.

Our infants and toddlers today are inundated with digital mobiles, electronic play stations that snap to the front of a stroller, and internet streaming in the back of car seats. One mother, who says she is not a morning person, puts on an educational streaming series for her 18-month-old toddler. More than two billion dollars a year is spent on electronic brain-boosters promising increased IQs. The only increases you can count on will be your budget and a greater loss of emotional relationship.

SO WHAT'S THE ANSWER

Nothing says do as I say, not as I do more than letting your children watch you in action. You can lecture them over and over again about what not to do, but it won't mean a thing when they see you doing the very opposite. Starting today, let's put down our smartphones when we're with our kids. Set the example.

Almost 80% of kids who say they have trouble falling asleep, report having daytime sleepiness issues, or even worse, say that they're woken during the night by an incoming text or a call. I recommend *not* allowing kids to use their smart phones as an alarm clock. It's too tempting to be drawn into checking their Facebook or e-mail accounts in the middle of the night. Get them a traditional alarm clock that requires them to get up and turn it off. Teach your kids how to get back into real life.

Also, know who your children are communicating with! Don't allow them to use encryption, secret passwords or text messages that automatically disappear. If your relationship is struggling and your children are hiding their online lives from you, it's time to dig in. You don't need permission to find out everything you want to know ! You need to get up to speed fast and see their posts, texts and who their friends are. If you do discover disturbing behavior, don't focus on what their consequences will be, but on the underlying weakness you have in your relationship. If you need additional professional help, don't be embarrassed to get it. As a clinician, parents are forever asking me if the benefits for young children using social media are worth it? Here's my short answer in the form of one of my favorite TV shows, *Shark Tank*. "I'm out!" When your child argues about going online to post, surf or play mindless video games, calmly rely on the expression "in our family" to underscore your limit setting and values. Don't cave! In the meantime here are some other common sense suggestions to increase the connection speed with your family.

- No smart phones until high school. (I know. Good luck.)
- No Facebook / Instagram or email until sophomore year in high school.
- No TV, cell phones or social media in bedrooms. Use alarm clock for morning wake-ups.
- No television, tablets or video use with children under the age of two.
- Limit digital tablet use with children under the age of five.
- No smart phones at dinner table, breakfast or lunch. Only conversation.
- No texting to family members while in the house. You must physically find them.
- No smart phones in certain social situations; Doctor's appointments, family discussions.

- Make sure you never text and drive. Never!
- If your children's friends come over to play, take all their cell phones away.

Finally, whether this millennial generation turns out to be the most resilient generation of all time, is a debate for a later time. For now, there's no debate that they are the most pampered and spoiled generation of all time. Millennial expectations are spreading fast and they are establishing themselves 'as a right for almost everything' including on college campuses. As an adjunct university professor, I have seen this trend coming for many years. The truth is, too many universities today don't even view their students as students anymore. They view them as customers and look for nonsensical ways to satisfy them as customers, from safe spaces to safe courses. It's all about cashflow, government subsidies to offset scholarships and fundraising. Each month you can find an educational column on this disturbing trend. If your child is not specializing in a professional field that requires an advanced degree or state licensing, you may want to consider another road while saving more than a hundred thousand dollars of student debt and encourage your graduate to move straight into the world of business internships.

Reset Tips

"The gift of your time will outlast any toy"
—MARY GORDON, ROOTS OF EMPATHY

1. ***Model problem-solving skills out loud.*** This is a marvelous strategy to allow a younger child a glimpse into how you solve your own problems. It works this way: Imagine you just finished a telephone call and need to figure out something based on that call. In a thinking-out-loud tone, you might say to yourself, *"Mmm, I wonder what is the best way to solve this. Let's see, I need to first make sure I have the time to go. I think I will look at my calendar first."* Children really pay attention to this kind of self-talk. It gives them an orderly sense of how thinking works and how calmly you work. You can also help your child practice this strategy for himself: *"Michael, let's figure this out together. Let me hear how you might solve fixing the brakes on your bike."*

2. ***Do not use your child's name at the beginning of a demand.*** *"Justin, you need to go to bed now."* Hearing his name in connection with a command is a trigger for a contest of wills. Instead, just say, *"It's 9:00. It is time to end our day and say goodnight."*

3. ***Keep compliments separate from negative feedback.*** "You cleaned your room well, *but* you forgot to make your bed." Your child will focus on hearing the word "but," and not take in your compliment.

4. ***Do the unexpected.*** Go bowling, miniature golfing, or to a park. Don't be predictable.

5. ***Talk about things that don't matter.*** If all you ever talk about are problems, you have a problem relationship. Start talking about things that aren't life-changing too. Laugh and have fun!

6. ***Don't point your finger.*** This degrading gesture of waving your finger shows a complete lack of respect. It makes a child feel powerless and diminished. When you want to make a point, use the proper tone of voice, vocabulary, or facial expression, instead of your finger.

7. ***Resist the 'why?' question.*** When a parent or teacher wants to use the "why" question it should be used with caution, especially if our tone of voice is off. To children 'Why?' stands for disapproval, disappointment, and displeasure.

    Even a simple "Why did you do that?" (at home or in a school setting) will likely evoke the memory and the feelings of, "Why in the world did you ever do something as stupid as that?" Often, when a parent asks the question "Why," the child will either adopt an answer which includes, "I don't know" (making a child again feel stupid), or it forces him to make up an answer (maybe even lie a little) that he thinks his parent or teacher wants to hear. Better to say, *"Tell me about it."*

8. ***Focus on positive outcomes.*** It allows the child to see a more successful outcome. "Take your bath right now, or there will be no food before bed" can be substituted by, "After you take your bath, I'll be happy to prepare your snack." "David, get in the car right now, or we won't be going to the bowling alley," can be substituted by, *"When we arrive at the bowling alley, I'll need your help in choosing the right ball."* This kind of language allows a child to visualize different behavior.

9. ***Don't talk in moments of high conflict.*** You may feel that anger helps get rid of your tensions, but it does not teach your child what he or she needs to learn. Calmly withdraw and say, *"In our family, we talk with respect. I know you can*

do that. I am going to the kitchen [backyard, living room, etc.]. Daniel, when you are ready, come and find me, and I will listen to every word you have to say."

10. **Memory lane.** From time to time look at old photo albums and old video clips of your child or teenager when his life was easier and happier. Children need to be reminded that their life hasn't always been this way. Listen for their spontaneous reactions. These images will provide serious clues to help them overcome the difficulties they are facing now.

11. ***Whenever possible, provide a heads-up announcement before making a change in plans.*** Children need time to change gears and adjust their expectations. Providing a heads-up an hour before, or even five minutes in advance, goes a long way in preventing a confrontation. For a change of plans such as pick-ups at school, or not going to a favorite place, it is best to inform the child the night before. In general, do not walk on eggshells in delivering any change-of-plans information. Be relaxed and just give the information. Do not show your child your apprehension. If your child reacts with anger, apply the Broken-Record technique *(See page 98)*. Do not get drawn into the child's attempt to control your plans.

12. ***Avoid asking a child "Did you?" (like a prosecutor) if you already know the answer.*** It encourages lying. Your child could think, "My mother or father must not know the answer if they are asking me." Then when you reveal that you do know, they will feel tricked and you will lose trust. Better to be direct and model truthfulness: *"David, I saw you push Michael."* Or, *"David, I know you took five dollars from my pants. If you need money come and see me and we will talk about it."*

13. ***Eliminate the word equal—substitute the word unique or special.*** For children who are part of large families they often feel someone is the favorite. When children feel they are lost among their brothers and sisters or their classmates,

it is helpful to say, *"Our relationship is one-of-a-kind in the whole world!" "Alex, there is only one you, and I love you in a very, very special way."*

Do not say, "I love everyone the same, or I love everyone equally." It cannot be true. You can divide money equally, but not emotion. Children will be very satisfied to learn that your love for them is unique, special and one-of-a-kind.

14. ***The thirty-second rule.*** When you want to correct or suggest a new way for a child to do something, keep it short—preferably within 30 seconds. Parents who talk too much weaken the message as well as themselves. Children interpret parents who talk too much as, "My parents would rather talk than act."

15. ***Do not let your child pressure you for an immediate answer.*** Spoiled children, as well as spoiled adults, do this to try to gain a quick favorable decision. It is highly manipulative. When you feel the pressure, say, *"I want to think it through before I give you my decision,"* or, *"I know you want a decision right now, but it would be unfair to give you an answer now. I know you understand,"* or, *"Let me give it some more thought."*

16. ***Don't force remorse!*** Don't force your child to say, "I'm sorry." Many children who have been overly punished feel removed from their feelings and conscience. It is best to wait until tensions calm down. Children are more likely to express their remorse then. It is better for them to say to a brother or sister, *"I was wrong for pushing you in the kitchen."* Or, *"I shouldn't have taken your magazine."* The words, *"I'm sorry"* are not nearly as important as hearing the heartfelt recognition of what you did.

17. ***The hand signal.*** If you can say it in 10 words, say it in five words. Don't nag, moralize, and lecture. Less talk and say more, or sometimes say nothing. From a distance, a quick hand signal showing a thumbs-up, or a nodding smile, can be very powerful, especially when other people are around.

Ask your child to invent a hand signal, so when you are in public together, he can be reminded of a habit or a helpful tip he may want to know about

18. ***Admit mistakes.*** It is simple enough to do, but few parents do this routinely. When you lose your temper, or make a mistake, apologize and be specific: *"Brian, I lost control of myself last night when I was putting you to bed. I was wrong to call you a bad name and make fun of you. I am so sorry. It will not happen ever again."* Modeling how to admit a mistake will show your child what happens when you own up to personal responsibility. (*A culture of truth*)

    This can also be very effective when a spouse does this in front of their child to make amends with a spouse. Children change faster when they see a parent change. *"Honey, I over-reacted in anger when you asked me to go upstairs and bring you your robe. I'm so sorry."*

19. ***Whisper voice.*** When you want to put special emphasis on a positive moment, move in very close to your child's ear (about three inches) and, with an extra soft and whisper-like voice, tell your child, *"I'm really enjoying being with you now."* Your whisper tone will travel right into your child's heart. One word of caution: Find a private moment. Be sure you do not do this in front of another child, as it will be an obvious trigger for jealousy. Another whisper expression can be, *"I like the way you are controlling yourself."*

20. ***The compliment alert.*** Children with low self-worth have difficulty taking in positive feedback. Here's the antidote: *Before* giving your child a compliment, alert him first to what's coming: *"Andrew, do you mind if I tell you something really good that you did?"* Wait for your child's response, and watch his face light up. If you don't give a heads-up, he may think, "Here comes another criticism." Adults who also have low self-worth will respond the same way. Be brief: Keep it under 30 seconds. Providing a good news alert allows time to switch mindsets.

21. ***Write notes.*** This is a marvelous way to show your child you think about them when they are not just in front of you. Use the right adjectives and colorful expressions. Let them find your notes in backpacks and pockets. *"I can't wait to see you when you come home from school. I have a yummy dinner for you. Your favorite."* Or, *"No question, today is going to be a better day!"*

22. ***Overhearing.*** Let your child overhear you talking on the phone with others about her in positive ways. Be sure your words are always specific, approving and enthusiastic. Be animated, but do not go overboard. Children listen in a riveted way when you are on the phone because this is one measure of "real intel" about what's going on in and outside of the family.

    "Do you know what Gregg did today? He stayed calm all morning and successfully controlled his temper. What a pleasure it was to be with him." This works especially well with grandparents and extended family members.

23. ***Learn the language of play.*** Children express their feelings through play the way adults mostly express their feelings through words. Parents mistakingly think of playing with their children as a constant state of teaching: "Look how this is done!" "Look where this goes!" "Do it this way — see, it works better!"

    Parents should follow their child's ideas and advance his/her "story" line during play. That means that the child gets to make up the rules and select whatever toy(s) he wants to use or give you. If you're not sure what to do, just ask in a very soft whisper voice, *"Jonathan, what should I do with this?"* I guarantee your child will tell you exactly what to do, and where to do it. Children engage primarily in three kinds of play: play for fun, play for mastery and play to work through psychological problems. While board games, backgammon, chess, and checkers can be fun, we need to be careful not to set up a climate of constant competition in the home. One way to change the climate is to allow the child to set the level of play by asking, *"How do you want me to play — hard, easy or medium?"*

Reset Tips

The best kind of play with a child is one that encourages spontaneity, creativity and freedom. Choose toys that lead to creative play (for example, drawing, clay, exploring, Lego™). Skip activities and games with pre-set rules, like board games.

24. ***Pre-arranged 'private time.'*** Life is busy. To help us stay organized sometimes we set-up pre-arranged times to play and bond with our children. Is that good? While one-on-one time is always great, parents need to know that continuous pre-arranged 'private time' often fails, not because kids didn't have fun, but because it didn't yield the deep emotional bonding that parents were looking for. You can't force a child to emotionally open-up on cue and on time. Kids, especially older ones, need to express themselves in spontaneous ways, and having a set time makes them feel like they have a doctor's appointment. *"Lilly, every Wednesday at 7:30 after dinner, will be our private time together."* Still, if that's the best you can do, by all means do it. Some time is better than no time. Other ways to say it might include, *"Lilly, this week we will do something alone, just you and me. Should we plan the day and time now, or play it by ear? For sure we will spend time alone together."*

25. ***The #1 Bully App.*** Although I strongly recommend not giving your middle schooler a cell phone, if you can't resist doing so, at least download an app that can make a world of difference when they are at school. *The Bully Alert Plus*™ is a powerful App that sends out a text alert or e-mail in real-time alerting an assigned school official that your child has been bullied, has witnessed bullying, or has experienced any other social issue that bothers them. Most students are too embarrassed to walk in the front office of their school to report a problem. They do not want to be seen by other students Now, with one-click, the school finds the student who sent the alert (very discreetly) and takes action

immediately on their behalf. It's easier for students to report an issue if they know the right adult in charge will make the first contact.

Students who use the Bully Alert Plus™ will boost their self-confidence and will have fewer incidents in the future. Students can also use The Bully Alert Plus™ for academic struggles, classroom issues, sports or other social issues without feeling embarrassed. It is easier to text, than to speak up or speak out in front of others. The alert has a pre-written message to reduce stress; although it can be edited too. Download it now on your child's phone.

iPhone™ *only.*

Five Rules Summary

Parents teach in the toughest school in the world.
The school for making people.
—VIRGINIA SATIR

We can't predict the future, but we can predict a relationship. When we apply the five parenting rules, they satisfy our three most important relationship needs: *Understand me, Accept me, Believe in me*. At the same time, it makes no difference how well we follow them if our tone of voice, facial expressions and body language betray our words with looks of sarcasm or impatience. No one wants to listen or cooperate when we look or sound arrogant, negative, a know-it-all, sarcastic, singsongy, too loud or controlling. You can feel a look much more powerfully than words.

Finally, don't keep looking for light-bulb moments, especially if you are in the "repair" phase of your relationship. Instead, focus on the long game. With that in mind, here's a snapshot summary that will transform all parenting relationships and the five life-skills children will acquire as a result.

RULE ONE

BUILDS EMPATHY

SHOW A COMPLETE UNDERSTANDING

- COLLECT
- CALIBRATE
- SUMMARIZE BACK
- CONFIRM

Experience tells us you can only help someone get over their feelings by helping them get through them, not get around them. It's not enough to know you understand, or even feel it, you must know how to show it to the satisfaction of another. What makes this so critical is that when you don't know how to fully show understanding to your child (or anyone else you care about), it is unlikely you will be the one they trust to help them with their life issues. Without a consistent feeling of being deeply understood, we are drawn to other connections and increase risky behaviors.

It's not about fixing anything. It's about being able to stay in the moment wherever it leads. You don't have to agree with what you hear, but you do have to communicate you believe what you are being told or what you see. Only when we are sincerely believed and taken seriously, do we begin to trust, relax and open-up.

Five Rules Summary

RULE TWO

BUILDS SELF-WORTH

TALK WITH RESPECT

- KEEP YOUR MELODY HUMBLE
- TALK WITH ADMIRATION
- SHOW UNCONDITIONAL ACCEPTANCE
- SHOW HEARTFELT APPRECIATION

Speaking with respect has a gracious and elegant tone about it. If I had to describe in a single idea what is meant by talking with respect, it would be consistently making the other person feel admired, and with status, especially during times of conflict.

RULE THREE

BUILDS SELF-AWARENESS

PROMOTE A FAMILY CULTURE OF TRUTH

- MODEL SELF-AWARENESS & SELF-CORRECTION
- KEEP YOUR MELODY HUMBLE
- GIVE FEEDBACK FREQUENTLY AND SPONTANEOUSLY
- NEVER EXAGGERATE
- EXPRESS APPRECIATION

Honest feedback is the hallmark of a great relationship. Promoting a family culture of truth teaches three stunningly important life skills: how to know ourselves, how we affect others and how to see the truth about others. Before we can change something, we must become aware of it.

A family culture of truth should be modeled and promoted every day as a core value, as you would hard work or a religious belief. Receiving valuable feedback with an open-mind is a central characteristic of maturity. When we model honest feedback given with respect and humility, we build trust and self-awareness.

RULE FOUR

BUILDS SELF-CONTROL

ENFORCE CON-SEQUENCES CONSISTENTLY

- KEEP YOUR MELODY HUMBLE
- BE CONSISTENT
- WHEN YOU MAKE A REQUEST, ASK ONLY ONCE
- EXPRESS APPRECIATION AFTER COMPLETION

Of all five parenting rules, parents struggle the most with enforcing consequences. They struggle primarily in three ways: not following through consistently, showing anger or upset too quickly and not knowing which consequence fits what situation.

I cannot overemphasize the importance of controlling your temper and remaining elegant when you enforce a consequence. *Never match your child's intensity,* especially if your child is already high-strung and wound tight. If you don't, you diminish your child's motivation to examine their own behavior and instead will draw their attention back to you in order to satisfy their need for retaliation. Finally, don't set a limit you can't enforce.

Five Rules Summary

RULE FIVE

BUILDS SELF-CONFIDENCE

SHOW UNRELENTING OPTIMISM

- SHOW A CALM POSITIVE ENERGY
- RECOGNIZE ALL EFFORT
- EXPRESS ENCOURAGEMENT, NOT PRAISE
- SHOW AN UNRELENTING DEEP BELIEF

The fifth and final parenting rule fulfills our last relationship need — *believe in me.* Expressing unrelenting optimism allows a child who hesitates for a moment to see a different outcome. After all, if you are consistently calm and positive, you must really believe everything will work out, even though it may not. *"I was just thinking about all the ways I respect and trust you."* Optimistic people makes us feel that something great is always about to happen. Receiving positive emotional energy fuels our motivation to develop our talents and face our struggles.

Remember, attitudes are contagious.

NOTES

NOTES

NOTES

NOTES

NOTES